博古通今学汉语丛书
Gems of the Chinese Language Through the Ages

The Stories Behind 100 Chinese Idioms

周荅仲
何泽人　编、译

李士伋　绘　图

华语教学出版社
SINOLINGUA

First Edition 1999
Ninth Printing 2012

ISBN 978-7-80052-522-3
Copyright 1999 by Sinolingua Co., Ltd
Published by Sinolingua Co., Ltd
24 Baiwanzhuang Road, Beijing 100037, China
Tel: (86) 10-68320585   68997826
Fax: (86) 10-68997826   68326333
http://www.sinolingua.com.cn
E-mail:hyjx@sinolingua.com.cn
Facebook: www.facebook.com/sinolingua
Printed by Beijing Mixing Printing Co., Ltd

Printed in the People's Republic of China

出版者的话

典故对于语言和文字的精炼和美化作用是众所周知的。了解典故的内容和来源，不仅对外国人，便是对某些知其然不知其所以然的中国人恰当地运用典故来说，也是有意义的。

本书是由周苓仲先生与其表兄何泽人先生编写、翻译的。一百则典故中，何泽人先生完成二十篇，周苓仲先生完成八十篇。

周先生与何先生退休前均为高级技术研究人员，并不专门从事语言文字工作；然而他们两人都出身于对中国文化有深刻了解，同时又熟悉英美文化的家庭。他们从小受到家庭文化气氛的熏陶和良好教育，在中、英文方面均学养有素，对祖国文化遗产怀有一腔热忱。

另外，周先生、何先生几十年来均生活、工作在陕西省渭水流域的西安、临潼、泾阳等地。渭水流域这片中国古代文化的重要发源地，那些产生过多少传世典故的名城、古迹，曾经给予他们怎样的影响是不言而喻的。

1995 年初，年逾古稀、健康欠佳的何泽人先生出于帮助外国人学习汉语、介绍中国文化的美好意愿，向中国翻译工作者协会的《中国翻译》编辑部提出编写这本书的计划并付诸实施；不幸只写了一部分便因病去世了。病重时，何先生将未竟之事嘱托给其表弟周苓仲先生，周先生慨然承诺。

后来,书稿转到华语教学出版社,周先生与我们再次商榷书的编写原则。他科学地排列了条目顺序,孜孜矻矻,历时半年,终于完成全部书稿;并将何先生所写的那部分加以充实、完善,圆满地实现了表兄的遗愿。

1999 年 4 月 5 日

Publisher's Note

Idioms serve to refine and beautify all languages. So it is helpful both for foreign students and native speakers of languages to learn to use these allusions appropriately. But to do so, they must know the origins and implications of the idioms.

This book was written and translated into English by Mr. Zhou Lingzhong and his cousin, the late Mr. He Zeren. Of the 100 idioms presented here, Mr. He worked on 20, and Mr. Zhou completed the rest.

Before their retirement the two compilers were senior technicians and research fellows. They had never specialized in literary work, but they came from a family which, steeped in Chinese culture, was at the same time well acquainted with the cultures of Britain and the United States of America. So the authors brought to this work a wide knowledge of both the English and Chinese cultures and languages, as well as a strong attachment to the rich cultural heritage of their motherland.

Mr. He and Mr. Zhou lived and worked for decades in Xi'an, Lintong and Jingyang, in Shaanxi Province, and in the Wei River Valley — all major cradles of Chinese culture. It is not hard to imagine how these famous ancient cities with their plethora of cultural relics, which gave rise to a multitude of popular tales and allusions, influenced them and gave them inspiration.

In 1995, Mr. He Zeren, though in poor health and advanced in years, proposed to the editors of *Chinese Translation* that this book be compiled in order to help foreigners better understand Chinese culture. Unfortunately, illness overtook him not long after the work began. On his sickbed, Mr. He entrusted the task to his cousin, and Mr. Zhou took it up readily.

Later, the manuscript was forwarded to Sinolingua, and Mr. Zhou collaborated closely with us in the further stages of its publication. He re-arranged the contents and enriched the parts written by Mr. He. After six months of diligent work the manuscript was completed, and thus the last wish of his dear cousin was fulfilled.

April 5, 1999

前　　言

中国有五千年文明史，有世界上最多的人口，然而中国语言，或者范围小些是汉族语言——汉语，并未被外国人广泛学习。这种情况妨碍了他们与中国在文化及其它方面的交流。

外国人对汉语了解甚少的原因之一，是汉语相当复杂，特别是古汉语和文言文。其中的许多引语和典故，有不少现在还在使用，不懂这些就会导致误解。我偶尔读过几篇中国古文的英译出版物，很遗憾地发现其中的一些错译，明显的是由于误解了原文中的引语和典故。

显然，现在有必要做些事来帮助外国人学汉语，特别是不同体裁的中国古文。我虽然只是中国文学和语言知识的爱好者，但是仍然愿意尽力做些工作，与海外华人和说英语的朋友们共享这方面的知识，因此编了这本小书。希望它对帮助读者学习汉语能起一些作用。

何泽人
1995 年 1 月 31 日

Preface

China has a history of 5, 000 years of civilization, and the largest population in the world; yet her language, or in a narrower sense, the language of the Han nationality, has not been widely studied by foreigners. This places impediments in the way of cultural and other types of communication between China and the outside world.

The Chinese language is a rather difficult one, which is one of the reasons why foreigners often fail to have a profound understanding of it. This is especially the case with the learning of the Chinese classics or writings in archaic Chinese. A lot of literary quotations and allusions are used in them, and many are still used nowadays. Ignorance of these is a prime cause of misunderstanding. I happened to have read a few English translantions of classical Chinese, and was sorry to find some mistakes in the translation which were obviously due to incorrect comprehension of the Chinese literary quotations and allusions in the original.

It is clear that more ought to be done to help foreigners learn Chinese, especially the Chinese classics in their various forms. Though I am only an amateur in Chinese literature and language, I would like to do my best in this field to share my knowledge with overseas Chinese and English-speaking friends by producing this small book. I hope that it will be of some use in clearing away the obstacles in the way of international understanding.

He Zeren
Jan. 31, 1995

目 录
Contents

出版者的话··· *1*

Publisher's Note··· *3*

前言··· *5*

Preface·· 6

1. 割鸡焉用牛刀··· 1
   Why Use a Poleaxe to Kill a Chicken?

2. 苛政猛于虎··· 4
   Tyranny Is Fiercer Than a Tiger

3. 伐柯··· 7
   Shaping an Axe Handle

4. 多行不义必自毙··· 9
   Persisting in Evil Brings Self-Destruction

5. 退避三舍··· 12
   Withdrawing for Three *She*

6. 假途灭虢　唇亡齿寒····································· 15
   Borrowing a Shortcut to Crush Guo
   When the Lips Are Gone, the Teeth Will Be Cold

7. 问鼎··· 18
   Asking About the Tripods

8. 染指··· 21
   Dipping a Finger Into the Pot

9

9. 鞭长莫及 ················· 23
Not Even the Longest Whip Can Reach Everywhere

10. 尔虞我诈 ················· 26
You Fool Me and I Cheat You

11. 余勇可贾 ················· 29
Surplus Strength for Sale

12. 上下其手 ················· 31
Raising and Lowering the Hand

13. 管鲍之交 ················· 34
The Friendship Between Guan and Bao

14. 风马牛不相及 ················· 37
Even the Runaway Livestock Would Not Reach Each Other

15. 结草衔环 ················· 39
Knotting Grass and Holding Rings in the Mouth

16. 顾左右而言他 ················· 43
Turning Aside and Changing the Subject

17. 坐山观虎斗 ················· 46
Sitting on a Hill Watching Tigers Fight

18. 狡兔三窟 ················· 49
高枕无忧
A Wily Hare Has Three Burrows
Shake Up the Pillow and Have a Good Sleep

19. 危如累卵 ················· 54
势如累卵
As Precarious as a Stack of Eggs

20. 前倨后恭 ················· 57
Haughty Before and Reverent Afterwords

21. 作法自毙··· 61
Hoist With His Own Petard

22. 奇货可居··· 64
A Rare Commodity Suitable for Hoarding

23. 逐客令··· 67
Order for Guests to Leave

24. 一字千金··· 70
One Word Worth a Thousand Pieces of Gold

25. 燕雀焉知鸿鹄之志································· 73
How Can a Swallow Know the Aspirations of a Swan?

26. 取而代之··· 75
Oust Him and Take His Place

27. 先发制人··· 78
Gain the Initiative by Striking First

28. 一败涂地··· 81
A Defeat That Brings Everything Crashing Down

29. 孺子可教··· 84
The Child Is Worth Instructing

30. 壁上观··· 87
Watching the Battle From the Ramparts

31. 成也萧何，败也萧何······························ 90
Raised Up by Xiao He and Cast Down by Xiao He

32. 逐鹿中原··· 93
Hunting Deer in the Central Plains

33. 约法三章··· 96
Agreeing on a Three-Point Law

34. 鸿门宴··· 99

项庄舞剑,意在沛公 ············ 99
The Banquet and Sword Dance at Hongmen

35. 人为刀俎,我为鱼肉 ············ 103
The Are the Knife and the Chopping Block, While
We Are the Fish and the Meat

36. 明修栈道,暗度陈仓 ············ 105
Repairing the Road While Making a Secret Detour

37. 背水一战 ············ 108
Fighting With One's Back to the River

38. 匹夫之勇 ············ 111
妇人之仁
Reckless Courage and Feminine Benevolence

39. 养虎遗患 ············ 114
To Rear a Tiger Is to Court Calamity

40. 衣锦夜行 ············ 117
Walking at Night in Silken Robes

41. 沐猴而冠 ············ 120
A Monkey With a Hat On

42. 韩信将兵,多多益善 ············ 122
The More Troops Han Xin Commands, the Better

43. 无面目见江东父老 ············ 125
Too Ashamed to Face the Elders East of the Yangtze

44. 运筹帷幄 ············ 128
Manipulating Victory From the Command Tent

45. 狡兔死,走狗烹 ············ 131
When the Crafty Hares Have Been Exterminated,
the Hunting Dogs Will Be Cooked

46. 羽翼已成 ················· 134
The Wings Are Fully Grown

47. 萧规曹随 ················· 137
Cao Can Follows Xiao He's Rules

48. 左袒 ····················· 140
偏袒
Loosening the Left Sleeve

49. 金屋藏娇 ················· 143
Keeping a Beauty in a Golden House

50. 门可罗雀 ················· 145
You Can Catch Sparrows on the Doorstep

51. 牛郎织女 ················· 148
鹊桥
The Cowherd and the Weaving Girl
Building a Bridge of Magpies

52. 鹏程万里 ················· 151
The Roc Flies Ten Thousand *Li*

53. 鼓盆之戚 ················· 154
The Sorrow of Drumming on the Basin

54. 相濡以沫 ················· 157
Moistening Each Other With Soliva

55. 每下愈况 ················· 159
每况愈下
The Lower, the More Accurate the Comparison Is

56. 枯鱼之肆 ················· 162
Dried Fish Market

57. 庖丁解牛 ················· 165
游刃有余

Butchering an Ox

Having Plenty of Room for the Play of the Butcher's

Cleaver

58. 徒劳无功 ·· 168

劳而无功

Working Hard But to No Avail

59. 视为畏途 ·· 171

Regarded as a Dangerous Road

60. 越俎代庖 ·· 173

Abandoning the Sacrificial Vessels for the Saucepans

61. 得心应手 ·· 176

The Hands Respond to the Heart

62. 泼水难收 ·· 179

Spilt Water Cannot Be Retrieved

63. 死灰复燃 ·· 181

Dying Embers May Glow Again

64. 投笔从戎 ·· 184

Exchanging the Writing Brush for the Sword

65. 不入虎穴,焉得虎子 ······································· 187

You Must Enter the Tiger's Den to Catch His Cubs

66. 马革裹尸 ·· 190

A Horsehide Shroud

67. 小巫见大巫 ··· 192

A Junior Sorcerer in the Presence of a Great One

68. 举案齐眉 ·· 195

Holding the Tray Up to the Eyebrows

69. 提刀 ·· 197

Holding the Sword

14

70. 万事俱备,只欠东风⋯⋯⋯⋯⋯⋯⋯⋯⋯⋯ 200
All That Is Needed Is an East Wind
71. 鹤立鸡群⋯⋯⋯⋯⋯⋯⋯⋯⋯⋯⋯⋯⋯⋯⋯ 203
Like a Crane Standing Among Chickens
72. 乐不思蜀⋯⋯⋯⋯⋯⋯⋯⋯⋯⋯⋯⋯⋯⋯⋯ 205
So Happy That One Thinks No More of Shu
73. 不为五斗米折腰⋯⋯⋯⋯⋯⋯⋯⋯⋯⋯⋯⋯ 207
Won't Kowtow for Five *Dou* of Rice
74. 桃花源⋯⋯⋯⋯⋯⋯⋯⋯⋯⋯⋯⋯⋯⋯⋯⋯ 210
Land of Peach Blossoms
75. 一人得道,鸡犬升天⋯⋯⋯⋯⋯⋯⋯⋯⋯⋯ 213
When a Man Attains the *Dao*, Even His Pets Go to
Heaven
76. 沧海桑田⋯⋯⋯⋯⋯⋯⋯⋯⋯⋯⋯⋯⋯⋯⋯ 215
Seas Change Into Mulberry Orchards and Mulberry
Orchards Into Seas
77. 阿堵物⋯⋯⋯⋯⋯⋯⋯⋯⋯⋯⋯⋯⋯⋯⋯⋯ 218
"Those Things"
78. 白面书生⋯⋯⋯⋯⋯⋯⋯⋯⋯⋯⋯⋯⋯⋯⋯ 220
Pale-Faced Scholars
79. 洛阳纸贵⋯⋯⋯⋯⋯⋯⋯⋯⋯⋯⋯⋯⋯⋯⋯ 222
Paper Is Expensive in Luoyang
80. 朝秦暮楚⋯⋯⋯⋯⋯⋯⋯⋯⋯⋯⋯⋯⋯⋯⋯ 224
Serving Qin in the Morning and Chu in the Evening
81. 东床⋯⋯⋯⋯⋯⋯⋯⋯⋯⋯⋯⋯⋯⋯⋯ 226
东床快婿
袒腹东床
Sprawled in the East Wing

82. 覆巢之下无完卵 ⋯⋯⋯⋯⋯⋯⋯⋯⋯⋯ 229
   No Intact Egges Under an Overturned Nest
83. 口若悬河 ⋯⋯⋯⋯⋯⋯⋯⋯⋯⋯⋯⋯⋯ 232
   A Waterfall of Words
84. 青眼 ⋯⋯⋯⋯⋯⋯⋯⋯⋯⋯⋯⋯⋯⋯⋯ 234
   青睐
   白眼
   Black Glances, White Glances
85. 江郎才尽 ⋯⋯⋯⋯⋯⋯⋯⋯⋯⋯⋯⋯⋯ 236
   Mr. Jiang Has Exhausted His Talents
86. 红绳系足 ⋯⋯⋯⋯⋯⋯⋯⋯⋯⋯⋯⋯⋯ 238
   月下老人
   Feet Linked by Red Cords
   The Old Man in the Moonlight
87. 阮囊羞涩 ⋯⋯⋯⋯⋯⋯⋯⋯⋯⋯⋯⋯⋯ 241
   Mr. Ruan's Bag Feels Ashamed
88. 司空见惯 ⋯⋯⋯⋯⋯⋯⋯⋯⋯⋯⋯⋯⋯ 243
   A Common Sight to the Sikong
89. 请君入瓮 ⋯⋯⋯⋯⋯⋯⋯⋯⋯⋯⋯⋯⋯ 245
   Please Get Into the Vat
90. 梨园 ⋯⋯⋯⋯⋯⋯⋯⋯⋯⋯⋯⋯⋯⋯⋯ 248
   Pear Orchard
91. 安乐窝 ⋯⋯⋯⋯⋯⋯⋯⋯⋯⋯⋯⋯⋯⋯ 250
   The Cosy Nest
92. 黄粱一梦 ⋯⋯⋯⋯⋯⋯⋯⋯⋯⋯⋯⋯⋯ 252
   A Golden Millet Dream
93. 南柯一梦 ⋯⋯⋯⋯⋯⋯⋯⋯⋯⋯⋯⋯⋯ 255
   Southern Branch Dream

94. 只许州官放火,不许百姓点灯 ····················· 258
Magistrates May Set Fires But Commoners May
Not Even Light Lamps

95. 冰人 ·· 260
The Iceman

96. 东窗事发 ·· 263
East Window Plot

97. 推敲 ·· 266
Push-Knock

98. 绿叶成荫 ·· 269
Green Leaves Make a Fine Shade

99. 红娘 ·· 272
Hongniang

100. 刘姥姥进大观园 ··································· 275
Granny Liu in the Grand View Garden

中国历史朝代年表 ································· 278
A Chronical Table of Chinese Dynasties

后记 ·· 282

Postscript ·· 283

割鸡焉用牛刀

gē jī yān yòng niú dāo

Why Use a Poleaxe to Kill a Chicken?

焉:哪里。　Why, how (in rhetorical questions).

此典出自《论(Lún)语》①。

孔子②有一个学生言偃(yǎn)在武成③做县令。有一次孔子到武成,听到弹琴和唱歌的声音。孔子以为在一个小城施行礼乐④没有必要,就笑对言偃说:"杀鸡哪里要用杀牛的刀(割鸡焉用牛刀)。"言偃分辩说,他进行礼乐教育正是遵照了老师的教导,而且这样做有利于治理武成。于是孔子承认言偃是对的,他说:"刚才的话只是一句玩笑。"

后世用"割鸡焉用牛刀"这句话来比喻小题大做或大材小用。

This story is taken from *Analects of Confucius*.

Yan Yan (言偃), a student of Confucius, was the magistrate of Wucheng (武成). Once when Confucius went there he heard the strains of zithers and the sound of singing. Deeming it extravagant to enact lavish ceremonies in such a small town, he said with a sardonic smile: "Why use a poleaxe to kill a chicken?" Yan Yan defended himself, saying that he was doing what his teacher had encouraged him to do, and thereby would govern Wucheng better. Then Confucius recognized the reason in Yan Yan's words, and said that he had only been joking.

Later, the metaphor "killing a chicken with a poleaxe" began to be used to describe making a fuss over a trifling matter, or wasting one's talent on a petty endeavor.

注:① 《论语》:孔子弟子关于孔子言行、思想的记录。为儒家经典。

Analects of Confucius (论语 Lún Yǔ), one of the Confucian classics, is a collection or record of the thoughts, words and deeds of Confucius compiled by his disciples.

② 孔子:(公元前 551—前 479) 春秋末期思想家、政治家、教育家,儒家的创始者。

Confucius (551-479 B. C.): the father of Confucianism, statesman, educationist and thinker in the Spring and Autumn Period.

③ 武成:今山东省费县西南。

In the southwest part of present-day Fei County, Shandong Province.

④ 礼乐:宣扬儒家政治思想和社会、道德规范的音乐及教育。

Music and rites that advocate Confucian political ideas along with social and moral code.

苛政猛于虎

kē zhèng měng yú hǔ

Tyranny Is Fiercer Than a Tiger

　　孔子经过泰山①旁边，听见有一个妇人在墓前哭得很伤心，就叫学生去问她说："你的哭声好像是有很重的哀伤。"她回答说："是的，从前我的公公被老虎吃掉，后来我的丈夫也被老虎吃掉，现在我的儿子也被老虎吃掉了。"孔子问她："为什么不离开这里呢？" 她回答说： "这里没有暴虐(bàonüè) 的统治(苛政)。"孔子回头对他的学生们说："年轻人记住，暴虐的统治比老虎更可怕(猛于虎)。"

　　后世用"苛政猛于虎"这句话来说明当政者不可暴虐，或者指责某处的统治者压迫人民。

Confucius was once passing by Mount Tai (泰山), when he heard a woman, who was standing in front of a grave, wailing bitterly. He sent one of his disciples to enquire the reason. "By the sound of your lamentation, " he said, "you seem to be afflicted by some grievous sorrow. " The woman replied, "Yes, a tiger killed and devoured my father-in-law, and then my husband suffered the same fate. Now my son has been gobbled up by another tiger. " Hearing this, Confucius asked her, "Then why don' t you leave this place?" The woman answered, "Because here there is no tyrannical rule. " Thereupon, Confucius turned to his disciples and said, "Keep this in mind, young fellows: tyranny is fiercer than a tiger. "

Later, this saying came to be used to warn rulers not to

act in a tyrannical fashion and to criticize governments which oppress their people.

注:① 泰山是中国的名山之一,在山东省。
Mount Tai is one of China's most famous mountains, situated in Shandong Province.

伐柯

fá kē

Shaping an Axe Handle

伐:砍。 To hew.

柯:斧子的柄。 (Axe) handle.

《诗经·豳(Bīn)风·伐柯》①一章说："怎样砍出斧柄呢？没有斧头就砍不出来。怎样娶到妻子呢？没有媒人就娶不到。"后世按这个比喻称做媒为"伐柯"，称媒人为"伐柯人"。

The stanza "Shaping an Axe Handle" in the "Songs of Bin" in the *Book of Songs* goes: "How does one shape an axe handle? It cannot be done without an axe. How does one marry a wife? It cannot be done without a matchmaker." Later, based on this metaphor, matchmaking came to be called "shaping an axe handle," and matchmakers came to be called "axe handle shapers."

注：① 《诗经》：周代到春秋时代编成的诗集。部分为官僚和知识分子(fènzǐ)所写，部分采集自民间，本诗即采自豳(Bīn)地。豳在今陕西省旬邑(yì)县附近。

The Book of Songs is a collection of poems, some written by aristocratic scholars and some being folk ballads, from the Zhou Dynasty to the Spring and Autumn Period. This poem is from the region of Bin which was near the present Xunyi County in Shaanxi Province.

多行不义必自毙

duō xíng bù yì bì zì bì

Persisting in Evil Brings Self-Destruction

此典出自《左传》①。

郑国国君寤（wù）生，于公元前743年即位，他的母亲不喜欢他而喜欢小儿子段，并且总想使段成为国君。她一再强求国君将一个重要城市京②，给段作为封地。段到京后一再扩建城墙，扩大自己的管辖范围。郑国的大夫劝国君及早除去段，以免因段的强大而危及郑国的安全。国君说："多行不义必自毙。"要大家等待。后来段聚集军队准备进攻郑的都城，国君说"到时候了。"于是发兵攻京，京地的人叛离了段，段只好逃到卫国。

后世以"多行不义必自毙"来形容做恶多了就会自取灭亡。

This anecdote is excerpted from the *Zuo Zhuan*.

The ruler of the State of Zheng (郑), Wu Sheng (寤生), succeeded to the throne in 743 B. C.. His mother did not like him, but dotted on her younger son Duan (段). She prevailed upon the ruler to give the major city of Jing (京) to Duan as his fief. After Duan obtained the city, he reinforced and heightened the city wall, and continuously expanded the area under his control. The ministers of Zheng warned the ruler that Duan was a threat to the stability of Zheng, and that he should take steps to eliminate him. But the ruler said, "He who persists in evil shall bring about his own destruction." He told his advisors to wait and see. Finally Duan gathered an army to attack the capital of Zheng. Wu

Sheng said, "The time has come, " and mustered an army to attack Jing. The people of Jing immediately deserted Duan, who fled to the State of Wei (卫).

Later, the expression "Persisting in evil brings self-destruction" was used to warn wrongdoers of the fate in store for them.

注：① 《左传》：相传由史学家左丘明所著。由此故事至第十五个故事都取材于《左传》。

Zuo Zhuan: *Master Zuo's Spring and Autumn Annals* covering the years 722-453 B. C. and is said to be written by Zuo Qiuming. Anecdotes 4 to 15 in this book are adapted from there.

② 京：古地名。在今河南荥(xíng)阳东南,距郑国都城很近。

Located in the southeast of Xingyang in present-day Henan Province, near the capital of Zheng.

退避三舍

tuì bì sān shè

Withdrawing for Three *She*

三舍：古时行军以三十里为一舍，三舍即九十里。

One *She* equalled 30 *li* (about 15 km) and was reckoned a day's march.

春秋时，晋国公子重（Chóng）耳为避难流亡在外。他到楚国时，楚王以诸（zhū）侯①礼仪接待重耳。有一次楚王问重耳："你将来回晋国做了国君，会怎样报答我呢？"重耳说："一切珍奇宝物你都有很多，我不知道还有什么更好的东西可以用来答谢你厚待我的情谊。"楚王还是坚持要求他说将怎样答谢。重耳说："以后万不得已要与你打仗，我将退避，让你三舍。"

后来，重耳回晋国做了国君。有一次楚国侵犯宋国，晋国应宋国请求与楚国交战。当楚军进攻时，重耳就命令他的军队后退三舍——九十里，遵守了从前的诺言。但楚军仍步步进逼，最后被晋军打得大败。

后世以"退避三舍"来表示对人有意退让或回避。

In the Spring and Autumn Period Prince Chong'er (重耳) was exiled from his native State of Jin (晋) and wandered from state to state for 19 years. When he went to Chu (楚), the ruler of Chu received him with the honor due to a fellow-ruler. One day the former asked Chong'er: "If you return to your own country some day and succeed to the throne, how will you reward me?" Chong'er replied: "Your Highness has a plenty of treasures; I do not know what would be worthy of being presented to Your Highness." When the ruler of Chu persisted, Chong'er answered, "Should I be forced some day to fight with the army of Your Highness on the battlefield, my troops would retreat for three *she* (舍) so as to express my gratitude to Your Highness."

Later, Chong'er did return to Jin and succeeded to the throne. An invasion by Chu upon the territory of the State of Song brought Jin into conflict with Chu because of Jin's alliance with Song. When the army of Chu launched an offense against his army, Chong'er ordered his men to retreat three *she*, i. e. 90 *li*, carrying out his promise made years before to the Lord of Chu. Chu pursued but suffered a crushing defeat in the end.

Later, the phrase "withdrawing for three *she*" came to be used to denote deliberately giving way or avoiding doing something in the face of superior strength.

注:① 诸侯:古代帝王统治下的列国君主的统称。

Dukes or princes under an emperor in ancient times.

假途灭虢

jiǎ tú miè Guó

Borrowing a Shortcut to Crush Guo

唇亡齿寒

chún wáng chǐ hán

When the Lips Are Gone, the Teeth Will Be Cold

假:借用。 To borrow.　　途:道路。 Road, way.

公元前 658 年,晋国给虞(Yú)国①送去很重的礼物,要求向虞国借路去攻打虢(Guó)国。虞国的一位大臣劝虞公说:"虞国和虢国的关系好像嘴唇和牙齿,嘴唇没有了,牙齿就要受冷,虢国亡了,虞国也存在不了。"但是虞公贪图礼物,同意了晋国的要求。结果晋国消灭了虢国之后,回军途中把虞国也消灭了。

后世以"假途灭虢"来比喻利用某人来损害别人,然后再损害被利用者。用"唇亡齿寒"来比喻关系密切的双方,一方受损另一方也要接着受损。

In 658 B. C. the State of Jin (晋) sent handsome gifts to the ruler of the State of Yu and asked that its army be allowed to take a shortcut through Yu's territory in order to attack the State of Guo. A minister of Yu advised his master not to allow this, saying, "Yu and Guo are like teeth and lips; when the lips are gone, the teeth will be cold. When Guo is annihilated, Yu will be the next victim." But the ruler of Yu coveted the gifts and consented. Consequently after the army of Jin annihilated Guo, it conquered Yu too on the way back.

Later, the phrase "borrowing a shortcut to crush Guo" came to mean to use somebody else to harm another and then to harm the former. The phrase "When the lips are gone, the teeth will be cold" is used as a metaphor to denote that when one side of a close relationship is removed, the other is in danger.

注:① 虞国和虢国是当时两个小诸侯国，地在今山西省平陆县及河南三门峡一带。

Yu and Guo were small states at that time, located in the area of the present Pinglu County in Shanxi Province and Sanmenxia（三门峡）in Henan Province, respectively.

问鼎

wèn dǐng

Asking About the Tripods

鼎：古代以为立国的重器，通常是三足两耳，青铜铸造。

A massive ceremonial bronze cauldron with three legs.

夏朝铸(zhù)了九个青铜鼎,列于朝廷之上作为王权的象征。夏亡后九鼎先后归商朝、周朝所有。

公元前 606 年,楚国军队在一次战争中进入周王治理的国土。周王派了一位官员去慰问楚王。楚王向这位官员打听九鼎的大小和重量。这位官员回答说:"周王朝虽然已经衰弱,但是上天给的治理国家的任命并未更改,所以关于鼎的情况是不能问的。"

后世用"问鼎"来比喻图谋夺取政权或力争某一领域的最高荣誉或地位。

Nine huge bronze tripods were cast during the Xia (夏) Dynasty, and exhibited in the royal court as symbols of supreme authority. When the dynasty fell, the cauldrons passed into the possession successively of the Shang (商) and Zhou (周) Dynasty kings.

In 606 B. C. the ruler of the State of Chu entered the territory of the King of Zhou, who was nominally the sovereign of all the Chinese states. When the king sent an official to greet the Chu ruler, the latter asked him about the size and weight of the nine tripods kept in the king's court. The official's reply was: "Though the Zhou Dynasty is declining, its mandate from Heaven to rule has not been removed. Therefore, no one may inquire about the condition of the tripods."

Later the phrase "asking about the tripods" came to denote a plot to obtain state power or to strive for the greatest honor or highest position in a certain field.

染指

răn zhĭ

Dipping a Finger Into the Pot

在公元前 605 年，楚国人送了一头大鳖 (biē) 给郑国的国君。郑君即命烹制，准备与贵族分食。郑国公子子公去见郑君时，食指跳动，他就对同行的子家说："我每逢食指跳动，就一定能尝到异味。"郑君知道了这件事，在分食大鳖时，却不分鳖肉给他。子公发怒，将手指浸入盛 (chéng) 鳖肉的鼎中，尝了沾在手指上的鳖汁就走了。郑君发怒要杀子公，但不久子公反而杀了郑君。

后世以"染指"来比喻沾取非分利益。

In 605 B. C. envoys from the state of Chu presented a giant turtle to the ruler of the State of Zheng. The latter ordered it to be cooked, and was going to share it with his nobles. On his way to the feast, Zi Gong (子公), an official of Zheng, felt his forefinger twitch. He said to his companion Zi Jia: "Whenever this happens it means that I'll surely have the chance to taste something extremely delicious." The ruler of Zheng heard about this, but gave Zi Gong no part of the turtle when it was served. Zi Gong was angry as well as hungry, so he dipped his finger into the tripod that held the cooked turtle, sucked the juice-stained finger, and left. The ruler of Zheng was so angry that he wanted to kill Zi Gong. However, he himself was slain by Zi Gong later in a coup d' etat.

Later, the expression "dipping a finger into the pot" came to mean taking a share of something one is not entitled to.

鞭长莫及

biān cháng mò jí

Not Even the Longest Whip Can Reach Everywhere

及:达到。To reach.

公元前 595 年,楚国派使臣去齐国,经过宋国时有意不通知宋国以示轻视。宋国杀了楚国的使臣,于是楚国发兵攻打宋国,两国相持很久不能分胜负。第二年,宋国请晋国发兵救援,但晋国的大夫(dàfū)①伯宗对晋国国君说:"马鞭子虽长,也不应打到马肚子上(虽鞭之长,不及马腹)。现在楚国正强盛,我们现在与楚国打仗是不利的,请你等待时机。"于是晋国只派了使臣告诉宋国不要投降楚国,晋国的救兵很快就到。但是实际上并未派兵。

后世以"鞭长莫及"来比喻力量达不到。

In 595 B. C. the State of Chu (楚) sent an envoy to the State of Qi (齐). As this man passed through the State of Song (宋), as an insult to that sovereign, he did not notify the Song ruler of his itinerary on purpose. As a result, the ruler of Song had the envoy executed, so Chu launched an attack on Song. But both sides were deadlocked. The following year, Song asked the State of Jin (晋) for help. A minister (大夫) of Jin, Bo Zong (伯宗) advised his ruler: "No matter how long a whip is, it cannot reach a horse's belly. Now Chu is strong, and so it is not advantageous for us to be at war with that state. Please wait until the time is ripe." Jin thereupon sent an envoy to Song to tell its ruler not to surrender, as reinforcements would arrive soon. But in fact none was sent.

Later, the expression "Even the longest whip cannot

reach everywhere" came to mean beyond the reach of one's power or authority, or too far away to send help.

注:① 大夫为古代官职。在国君之下有卿 (qīng)、大夫、士三级。

An official in ancient China. There were three ranks of officials, i. e. *qing* (卿), *dai fu* (大夫) and *shi* (士).

尔虞我诈

ěr yú wǒ zhà

You Fool Me and I Cheat You

尔:你。You.

虞:欺骗。To cheat, deceive.

公元前 594 年，楚国进攻宋国的军队已经在宋国停留了很久，但是不能取胜，于是楚军修建房子，开垦田地以示要长期作战。宋国感到害怕，于是宋国的将军华元夜间进入楚营，从床上把楚国统帅子反拉起来，告诉他宋国虽然已经很困难，但誓死不订立亡国条约，如果楚军后退三十里就可以讲和。楚军接受了这个要求而退兵。两国定了和约，盟誓说："我不骗你，你也不骗我"（我无尔诈，尔无我虞）。然后华元去楚国作人质，这场战争就结束了。

后世用"尔虞我诈"来形容人与人之间彼此猜疑、互相欺骗。

In 594 B. C. the army of the State of Chu (楚) attacked Song (宋) but couldn't win and found itself in a long-drawn-out campaign. The invaders began to build houses and cultivate land to show they were preparing for a long war. The ruler of Song was alarmed at this and sent Hua Yuan (华元), one of his senior generals, to steal into the Chu camp at night. Waking up Chu's commander-in-chief, Zi Fan (子反), Hua Yuan declared that though Song was in a desperate situation, its people would rather die than surrender. However, he said, if the army of Chu would retreat 30 *li*, peace could be made. Chu accepted the suggestion and retreated. Then a treaty was made by the rulers of Chu and Song and sealed with an oath to the effect that "I shall not fool you and you will not cheat me." Hua Yuan gave himself up to Chu as a hostage, and the war ended.

Later, this phrase was changed to the contrary, i. e. "You fool me and I cheat you." It is used to describe people who are suspicious of and cheat each other.

余勇可贾

yú yǒng kě gǔ

Surplus Strength for Sale

贾:卖。To sell.

公元前589年，齐国入侵鲁国，晋国发兵救鲁。两军对阵时，齐军的一个叫高固的将领冲入晋军，举石砸倒一晋兵，将其俘虏，并夺得他的兵车驾着回来。高固还在兵车后绑了一株带根的桑树，围着齐军营垒转，一面大喊："需要勇气的人快来买我剩余的勇气！（欲勇者，贾余余勇）。"

后世用"余勇可贾"来称赞某人的勇气过人，或力未使尽。

In 589 B. C. when the State of Qi (齐) invaded its neighbor Lu (鲁), the State of Jin (晋) sent an army to relieve Lu. Gao Gu (高固), a Qi general, charged into the army of Jin, struck a Jin soldier down with a rock, captured him and took his chariot. Gao Gu drove the chariot back, hitched an uprooted mulberry tree on it and drove it around the battle formation of the Qi army, shouting, "Whoever wants strength, come and buy what I have left!"

Later, the expression "surplus strength for sale" is used to mean still having plenty of fight left in one, or with strength to spare. It is often used to praise a man for excelling in courage and strength.

上下其手

shàng xià qí shǒu

Raising and Lowering the Hand

　　公元前 547 年，楚国攻打郑国。楚将穿封戌
(Xū)活捉了郑将皇颉(Xié)。在楚军中的贵族公子
围却要把这个功劳攫 (jué) 为己有。由于二人争
功，就请军中另一将军伯州犁裁处(chǔ)。伯州犁
说这事要问俘虏，于是把皇颉带来。伯州犁高抬起
手来向他说："这位先生是王子围，是我们国君尊
贵的弟弟，"又降下手说："这个人是穿封戌，是一
个外县的县官。他们二人中是谁俘虏了你？"皇颉
领会伯州犁的意图，说："我遇上了王子，被他打败
了。"这样功劳就归了公子围。

　　以后人们就用"上下其手"这个典故来形容某
些人玩弄手段、串通作弊，随意操纵事情发展。

　　In 547 B. C. the State of Chu (楚) invaded the State of
Zheng (郑). Chuanfeng Xu (穿封戌), a Chu general,
captured Huang Xie (皇颉), a general of the Zheng army.
But Prince Wei (围) of Chu wanted to take the credit for this
capture. Chuanfeng Xu and the prince decided to take their
dispute for arbitration to Bo Zhouli (伯州犁), another Chu
general. The latter demanded that the prisoner himself be
asked who had captured him. So Huang Xie was brought
forth. Bo Zhouli raised his hand, indicating Prince Wei, and
said, "This gentleman is Prince Wei, an honored younger
brother of our soveveign". Then he lowered his hand, indicating Chuanfeng Xu, and said, "This man is Chuanfeng
Xu, magistrate of an obscure county. Now, who captured

you?" The hint was not lost on Huang Xie, who answered, "I encountered the Prince and was defeated. " So Prince Wei got the credit for his capture.

Later, the allusion "raising and lowering the hand" is used to indicate resorting to tricks, collaborating in cheating and rigging outcomes.

管鲍之交

Guǎn Bào zhī jiāo

The Friendship Between Guan（管）and Bao（鲍）

管仲是春秋时著名的齐相,在他的治理下,齐国成为当时最强的诸侯国,并一度成为霸主。

从年轻时管仲和鲍叔牙就是好朋友。他们曾在一起经商,管仲经常私自多取财利,鲍叔牙知道以后认为管仲家贫而且要奉养老母,所以并不责怪管仲。管仲办事、做官累(lěi)次失败,鲍叔牙认为是由于时机不好,并不是管仲的过失。

后来管仲侍奉公子纠,鲍叔牙侍奉公子小白。在这两位公子争夺齐国权位时,小白取得胜利。于是纠被杀,管仲被囚禁。鲍叔牙知道管仲很有治国才能,就向齐桓公(小白)推荐管仲,说如果想成为霸主就必须任用管仲为相。齐桓公接受了这个意见。管仲为相后,地位还在鲍叔牙之上。七年以后齐国就成为各诸侯国的霸主。

管仲对人说:"生我的是父母,了解我的是鲍叔牙啊!"

后来用"管鲍之交"来形容朋友之间交谊深厚。

Guan Zhong (管仲) was a famous prime minister of the State of Qi (齐) in the Spring and Autumn Period. His administration made Qi the strongest state for a time and was the hegemon of all the states.

Guan Zhong and Baoshu Ya (鲍叔牙) were close friends from childhood. When they engaged in trade, Guan

Zhong often took more than his share of the profits, but Baoshu Ya didn't blame him because he took into account the fact that Guan Zhong was poor and had to provide for his aged mother. Guan Zhong failed again and again in various undertakings and in securing official positions. Baoshu Ya attributed these failures to unfavourable opportunities, and not to Guan Zhong himself.

Afterwards, Guan Zhong served Prince Jiu (纠) while Baoshu Ya served Prince Xiaobo (小白). These two princes fought for the throne, and Xiaobo won. Jiu was slain and Guan Zhong was imprisoned. Baoshu Ya knew Guan Zhong was a man of great political ability, so he recommended Guan Zhong to the new ruler, saying that if he wanted to be the hegemonic leader he should appoint Guan Zhong as his prime minister. The ruler accepted the suggestion. After Guan Zhong was thus appointed, his position was even higher than that of Baoshu Ya. After only seven years Qi became the hegemon.

Guan Zhong had often said: "I was begotten by my parents, but only Baoshu Ya really knows me."

Later, the phrase "the friendship of Guan and Bao" became used to describe a deep friendship with mutual understanding.

风马牛不相及

fēng mǎ niú bù xiāng jí

Even the Runaway Livestock Would Not Reach Each Other

风：一说是逃跑，走失；一说是兽类雌雄相诱。"Runaway, lost" in one version, and "enticement between male and female animals" in another.

公元前 656 年，齐国聚集各诸侯国的军队进攻蔡国，打败蔡国后又去侵犯楚国。楚国派了使者到齐军说："你们处在北海，我们处在南海，两地距离这么远，就是牛、马跑掉了也跑不到对方的地界去。你们干吗要到这里来呢？"齐国便找些借口说明自己征讨有理，而楚国表示自己虽然国力不强，却会誓死抵抗的。在楚国这种强硬态度面前，齐国和各诸侯国只好与楚国讲和，各自回国去了。

后世用"风马牛不相及"来表示人或事之间没有任何关系。

In 656 B. C. the State of Qi（齐）led a coalition of armies to attack the State of Cai（蔡）. After Cai was defeated, they invaded the State of Chu（楚）. Chu sent an envoy to the Qi army, who said, "Your homeland is by the north sea, and ours is by the south sea. Even runaway livestock could not reach the territory of the other. So what brings you all the way here?" The Qi side brought up some pretexts to justify their actions, but, as Chu showed itself resolved to resist, the two finally made peace and the coalition armies dispersed.

Later, "Even runaway horses and cattle would not reach each other" became used to describe the fact of having absolutely nothing to do with each other.

结草衔环

jié cǎo xián huán

Knotting Grass and Holding Rings in the Mouth

　　晋国大夫魏颗的父亲魏武子有个宠（chǒng）爱的妾，魏武子得病的时候曾对他儿子说："我死后你要把她嫁给别人"。后来魏武子病危了，又对魏颗说："一定要让她为我殉（xùn）葬①"。魏武子死后，魏颗就把那个妾嫁出去。他说："人到病重的时候神志就不清醒。我按我父亲头脑清醒时说的话去做。"后来魏颗与秦国将领杜回打仗，看见一个老人用草结成草把绊倒杜回，杜回因此被魏颗捉住。魏颗夜里梦见那老人说："我就是你嫁出去的那个妇人的父亲，因为你救了我女儿的命，今天特意来报恩。"

　　另外，南朝梁朝的笔记小说里记载：

　　汉朝时的杨宝九岁的时候，在华阴山北看见一只黄雀被鹞（yào）子抓伤，掉在树下，许多蚂蚁围困着它。杨宝就把它带回去饲养。过了些天，鸟的羽毛长好之后就飞走了。当夜有个穿黄衣服的童子，嘴里衔着四个白玉的环子，对杨宝拜谢，说："我是西王母②的使者，你这样仁爱地搭救我，十分感激，特来赠给你这些玉环，让你的子孙都像玉环一样洁白高尚，做到很高的官。"后来杨宝的儿孙后辈果然都做了大官。

　　后来人们常把"结草"和"衔环"连在一起说，比喻真心实意地感恩报德。

Wei Wuzi (魏武子), the father of Wei Ke (魏颗), an official of the State of Jin during the Spring and Autumn Period, had a favorite concubine. When the old man fell ill he instructed his son to marry her off to someone else in case of his death. But later, as his condition worsened, he told Wei Ke to kill her after he died and place her beside him in his grave so that they could be together in the afterlife. However, after his father's death, Wei Ke did not kill the woman, but let her remarry. He explained his action by saying, "When a person is sick to the point of death, he is not responsible for his words. I obeyed my father's will expressed when he was still of sound mind."

Later, when locked in heated combat with Du Hui (杜回), commander of an army of the State of Qin, he noticed a strange old man busily knotting tufts of grass on the battlefield. Du Hui's horse stumbled on one of the traps, and Du Hui was captured. That night Wei Ke dreamt that the same old man appeared to him, saying, "I am the father of the woman whose life you spared. I have repaid your merciful kindness."

A similar moral is contained in the story, *Holding Rings in the Mouth:*

During the Han Dynasty a nine-year-old boy named Yang Bao (杨宝) saw a flock of owls attacking a yellow bird. The yellow bird fell to the ground, whereupon it was attacked by ants. Yang Bao rescued the bird, took it home and took care of it. One day, when it was well again, the bird flew away. That same night Yang Bao dreamt that a boy clad all in yellow appeared to him holding four jade rings in his mouth. The apparition said, "I am a herald of the Western Queen Mother of the Gods. In return for your rescuing me, I present you with these rings. Your descendants will be as pure as these rings and will rise to high rank."

Sure enough, Yang Bao's son, grandson and great-grandson all became senior officials.

Later, the two expressions came to be used to denote expressing heartfelt gratitude.

注:① 殉葬：古代的一种风俗，逼迫死者的妻妾、奴隶等随同埋葬。

An ancient Chinese custom that concubines and servants were buried alive together with their deceased master.

② 西王母：中国古代神话中的女神，通称王母娘娘。

Goddess in ancient Chinese mytholody, usually called Wangmu Niangniang.

顾左右而言他

gù zuǒ yòu ér yán tā

Turning Aside and Changing the Subject

战国时齐宣王没有好好治理齐国。孟子①去见齐宣王，问他说："有一个人要出远门，把妻子托付给一个朋友。等他回来却发现妻子在冻饿之中。遇见这种事的人该怎么办呢？"

齐王说："该与这个有过失的朋友绝交。"

孟子又问："有一个狱官，连手下的属吏他都管不了。大家都认为他不称职。对这样的官员应当怎样处理呢？"

齐王说："该罢他的官。"

孟子再问："如果一个国家管理不好，又该怎么办呢？"

齐王不敢说该废黜（chù）这样的国王，就转向他的侍从（左右）讲别的事情去了。

后世用"顾左右而言他"或"王顾左右而言他"来形容某些人为避免答复问题或批评而去做别的事或岔开话题。

Mencius (孟子) was a great scholar in the Warring States Period (战国). In his time, King Xuan of Qi (齐宣王) was remiss in ruling his kingdom. Mencius went to the king and said to him: "There was a man who was about to go on a long journey. Before he left he entrusted his wife to a friend. But when he returned, he found his wife cold and starving. In such a situation, what should the man do?" The King answered, "He should break off all relations with such a friend. " Then Mencius said again: "There is a jailor who cannot control his subordinates and has a reputation for incompetence. What should be done in the case of such an officer?" The king said, "He should be dismissed from his post. " Mencius put a third question to the king: "Then what should be done when a kingdom is ill ruled?" The king dared not say that such a king should be dethroned, so he simply turned to his attendants and talked about something else.

Later, the phrase "turning aside and changing the subject" came to be used to describe the act of avoiding answering awkward questions or being criticised.

注:① 孟子: (约公元前 372—前 289) 名轲 (Kē), 山东邹
人。一度任齐宣王客卿。他是孔子以后最重要的儒
家领袖。

Mencius (C. 372-289 B. C.): surnamed Meng and named Ke, born in the State of Zou in present-day Shandong Province, he was an advisor of the King Xuan of Qi, and the most important representative of Confucianism after Confucius.

坐山观虎斗

zuò shān guān hǔ dòu

Sitting on a Hill Watching Tigers Fight

此典出自《战国策》①。

战国时期,韩、魏两国打仗,很久没有胜负,秦王拿不定主意应当采取什么行动。有一位谋士给秦王讲了卞 (Biàn) 庄子杀老虎的故事,他说:"有两只老虎在争吃一头牛,卞庄子要去杀这两只老虎,他的朋友阻止了他,说两只老虎为争牛肉必定要打起来,结果是小的被咬死,大的被咬伤,到那时就能轻而易举地杀死两只老虎。卞庄子果然等到老虎一死一伤之后,很容易地杀死了受伤的老虎,一举得到了两只老虎。现在韩、魏两国相争,到最后也必定是一亡一伤,那时你再去攻击,就能一举两得。"秦王按这个办法果然大获胜利。

后世把那谋士说的故事叫做"坐山观虎斗",以此比喻看着别人相斗,等到两败俱伤以后,再乘机插手取利。

This story is taken from the *The Records of the Warring States*.

In the Warring States Period the states of Han (韩) and Wei (魏) were at war and locked in a stalemate for a long time. The King of Qin (秦) was considering whether to become involved. One of his advisers told him the story of how Bian Zhuangzi (卞庄子) killed tigers. He said, "Once, Bian Zhuangzi saw two tigers fall upon an ox. He was just about to go and try to kill them when his friend stopped him, explaining that the tigers would fight over the ox; the smaller one would end up being killed, while the other would be badly wounded. If Bian Zhuangzi were to wait until then, he would take both tigers easily. Bian Zhuangzi did as he suggested. Just as expected, the smaller tiger was killed by the bigger one, which, being wounded, was killed easily by Bian Zhuangzi. So the two tigers were taken in one move. Now Han and Wei are at war. The result will be that one will be subjugated and the other weakened. If you attack then, you will gain both with one blow." The King of Qin accepted this suggestion and gained an easy victory.

　　Later, the expression "sitting on a hill watching tigers fight" came to be used to mean watching in safety while others fight, then reaping the spoils when both sides suffer.

注:①《战国策》是一本收集了战国时代政客们的计谋、言论的书。

　　The Records of the Warring States (战国策) contains anecdotes about political intrigues and stratagems during the Warring States Period (475-221 B. C.)

狡兔三窟

jiǎo tù sān kū

A Wily Hare Has Three Burrows

高枕无忧

gāo zhěn wú yōu

Shake Up the Pillow and Have a Good Sleep

齐国的丞（chéng）相孟尝君有一个叫冯谖（Xuān）的食客①，起先孟尝君并未重视他。有一次孟尝君要派人到封地薛去收债，冯谖自愿去做这件事。行前他问孟尝君要带什么东西回来，孟尝君说请冯谖买家中所缺的东西。冯谖到薛以后，将债务免除，债券都烧掉了。他回去以后向孟尝君说为孟尝君把"义"买回来了，孟尝君把事情问清楚以后很不高兴。一年之后，齐王免除了孟尝君的职务，于是他只得回到自己的封地薛。他还未到，薛地的老百姓就都出来迎接他。孟尝君对冯谖说："现在我才见到先生为我买的义。"冯谖说："狡猾的兔子有三个藏身的洞窟（狡兔三窟）才能免死。现在你只有一窟，还不安全，我去再为你掘两个窟。"于是冯谖到魏国说齐国把孟尝君免了官，谁要是先聘（pìn）请到他，就可以国富兵强。于是魏国派使者带了大量黄金和车马去请孟尝君来做魏国的丞相，去了三次孟尝君都拒绝了。齐王知道了这个消息，就派人去向孟尝君道歉，并且送去大量黄金和车马、佩剑，请他回去治理齐国。冯谖又教孟尝君要求齐王将先王的宗庙和祭器迁到薛。事成之后，他向孟尝君说："现在三窟都已掘好，你可以高枕无忧了。"孟尝君在齐国做了几十年丞相没有遇到危险，都是靠冯谖的计谋。

后世以"狡兔三窟"比喻给自己安排多处活动

余地以保证成功或安全。以"高枕无忧"说明一切
都平安。

Meng Changjun, the prime minister of the State of Qi
(齐), had a hanger-on named Feng Xuan (冯谖). Meng
didn't take him seriously at first. Then one day Meng wanted
to send a man to collect debts from his estate of Xue (薛).
Feng Xuan volunteered to go. Before his departure he asked
what he should bring back. Meng said that he should bring
back whatever he saw was lacking in the house. After Feng
Xuan arrived in Xue he remitted all the debts and burned all
the bonds. Then he returned and reported that he had
brought back "righteousness," which was lacking in the
house. When Meng understood what had happened, he was
quite vexed. The next year, the ruler of Qi relieved Meng
Changjun of his post, so he returned to Xue. The citizens of
Xue came a long way in crowds to greet him. He said to Feng
Xuan: "Now I see the 'righteousness' you brought for me."
Feng Xuan said, "A wily hare has three burrows to hide in.
But now, you have only one. You are not safe; I shall go and
dig another two for you." So Feng Xuan went to the State of
Wei (魏) and told its ruler that Qi had demoted Meng, and
that whoever engaged Meng's services would become rich
and powerful. So the ruler of Wei sent an envoy with a large
amount of gold and many chariots to ask Meng to be his prime
minister. The envoy visited him thrice, but was rebuffed
every time. When the ruler of Qi heard about this, he sent an

envoy with a large amount of gold, chariots and swords to ask Meng to return and administer the State of Qi once more. Then Feng Xuan advised Meng to ask the ruler to move the royal shrine and the sacrificial vessels to Xue. When this was done, Feng Xuan told Meng: "Now the three burrows are all prepared; you can shake up the pillow and have a good sleep." With Feng Xuan to advise him, Meng Changjun was premier of Qi for decades without getting into any danger.

Later, the metaphor "A wily hare has three burrows" came to be applied to somebody who prepares for any eventuality. "Shake up the pillow and have a good sleep" means that everything is safe, and so one can sit back and relax.

注：由此故事到第四十九个故事取材于《史记》。《史记》是汉代司马迁著的史书。约于公元前 104 年至前 91 年撰成。范围由远古到公元前 100 年，首尾共三千年左右。是中国古代最重要的史书，有很高的历史与文学价值。

Stories 17 to 49 are taken from the *Records of the Historian*（史记）by Sima Qian（司马迁）of the Han Dynasty. As the most important collection of chronicles in ancient China, it records historical events from remote antiquity to 100 B. C. — 3, 000 years in all. It has a very high historical and literary value.

① 食客：古代寄食在贵族官僚家里，为主人策划、奔走的人。

A person sponging on an aristocrat; a hanger-on of an
aristocrat.

危如累卵　　　　势如累卵

wēi rú lěi luǎn　　　　shì rú lěi luǎn

As Precarious as a Stack of Eggs

　　春秋时，晋灵公为了享乐，造一座九层高台，耗费千金，三年还没造成，国家的人力财力却耗尽了。他还说："谁敢谏(jiàn)阻我，就杀了他！"他的一位臣子荀息听到这事，就请求见灵公。灵公怒气冲冲地拿着弓箭与他相见。荀息说："我并不敢谏阻你。我能把十二枚棋子一个个累上去，上面再加九个鸡蛋。"灵公说："请你做给我看。"荀息就使自己安静镇定下来，专心一意地去做，把棋子摆在下面，上面加上九个鸡蛋。旁边看的人都很担心害怕，灵公也紧张得透不过气来。他说："危险哪！危险哪！"荀息说："这不算危险，还有比这更危险的呢！"他接着沉痛地说："你造九层的高台，三年不成。男的不能种地，女的不能织布，国家的财力都空虚了，邻国就会要来侵犯我们，国家将灭亡。这不是更危险吗？"灵公终于醒悟说："是我错了，我犯了这么大的错！"他立即下令停止造台，并表示悔过。

　　后世以"危如累卵"或"势如累卵"来比喻处境、形势非常危险。

　　In the Spring and Autumn Period the ruler of the State of Jin（晋）gave an order to build a nine-storey-high terrace as a pleasure resort. The construction had taken three years and was yet far from completion. Moreover, it was depleting the manpower and financial resources of the state. But the ruler

said, "He who dares to remonstrate shall be executed."
Having heard of this, one of the courtiers of Jin, Xun Xi (荀
息), requested an audience. The ruler granted him the in-
terview angrily, and sat on his throne with a bow and arrow in
hand. Xun Xi said, "I dare not try to dissuade Your Highness, but I wish to show you how I can pile up 12 chess
pieces one upon another, and add furthermore nine eggs, one
on top of the other on top of them." The ruler said, "Please
demonstrate." Xue Xi then calmed himself, and focussed his
mind. He piled up the chess pieces as he had said, and then
put nine eggs on top of them one on top of the other. All the
onlookers held their breath in suspense. The ruler was so
nervous that he felt suffocated. "That is most precarious," he
exclaimed. Xun Xi replied, "No, this is not really precarious. There is something even more precarious than this."
Xun Xi continued, "It has taken three years so far to build
the nine-storey terrace for Your Highness, and it is still not
complete. Men have given up farming, and women have
stopped weaving. The manpower and financial resources of
the state are virtually exhausted. As a consequence, neigh-
boring states are preparing to take advantage of our weakness
and attack us. Our state is about to perish. What could be
more precarious than that?" Thereupon, the ruler came to
realize his misconduct, and, after criticizing himself, gave
an order to halt the construction work.

   Later, the phrase "as precarious as a stack of eggs"
came to apply to an extremely dangerous situation.

前倨后恭

qián jù hòu gōng

Haughty Before and Reverent Afterwards

倨：傲慢。 Arrogant, haughty.

苏秦是战国时洛阳人。他到各国去游说①(shuì)了几年，但是没有人用他的计策，落得十分穷困回了家。他的父母不把他当儿子看待，他妻子坐在织布机上不起来迎接他，嫂子也不给他做饭吃，苏秦非常惭愧难过。于是他闭门发奋读书，过了一年又出去游说了。

这次他说服了六个国家的国君，使六国联合起来共同对抗秦国。苏秦当了这个联盟的首领，并佩带六国的相印回家，气派像个国王。他的父母打扫了房屋，修好了路，设了酒食，奏着乐，出城三十里外去迎接他。妻子不敢正面看他，侧着耳朵听他说话。嫂子在地上爬着走，对他一再跪拜谢罪。苏秦问她：“为什么从前那么傲慢，而现在这样恭敬呢？(何前倨而后恭也)”嫂子回答说：“因为你官高而且富有。”苏秦叹息说：“同样是我这个人，富贵时家人都怕我，贫贱时都看不起我，亲人都这样，何况别人。”

后世以“前倨后恭”表示某些人对人前后态度的不同。

Su Qin (苏秦) was a native of Luoyang (洛阳) during the Warring States Period. He had sought to become an adviser to the rulers of several states, but without success. Returning home in low spirits, he found that his parents treated him coldly, as if he were not their son; his wife sat at the loom and did not rise to greet him; and even his sister-in-law would not prepare meals for him. Mortified, Su Qin shut himself up in his room and devoted himself to his books. After a year he went travelling in search of employment again. This time, he managed to persuade the rulers of six states to form an alliance against the powerful and aggressive State of Qin. He himself was made prime minister of the alliance. Wearing the regalia of the prime minister of all the six states, Su Qin returned home with all the pomp and circumstance befitting his high rank. Hearing of his approach, his parents cleaned the house, rebuilt the local road, prepared wine and exotic dishes, and went out thirty *li* from the city to greet him with music. His wife dared not look him in the face. His sister-in-law crawled on all fours and kowtowed to him again and again to apologize for her former offence. Su Qin smiled and asked her, "Why were you so arrogant before and so humble now?" She answered, "It is because you hold a high position and have great wealth now." Su Qin sighed and said, "I am the same person as I was before. Now that I am rich and hold a high position, all my kin are in awe of me. But when I was poor and humble, they slighted me. If even my own kith and kin behave like this, how can I expect others to behave?"

Later, the phrase "haughty before and reverent afterwards" came to be used to indicate how people's attitudes toward one can easily change, depending on one's change of fortune.

注：① 游说：古代的政客奔走各国，凭着口才劝说君主采纳他的主张，叫做游说。

Go about selling an idea; go canvassing for employment. Philosophers and scholars in ancient China often travelled from state to state seeking to be employed as advisers to some ruler.

作法自毙

zuò fǎ zì bì

Hoist With His Own Petard

　　秦孝公时，政治家公孙鞅（Yāng）（约公元前390—前338）由魏国到秦国。他帮助秦孝公改革了法律，改变了落后的习俗，使秦国强盛起来。他担任丞相并被封于商，故称商鞅。商鞅被太子和许多秦国的贵族敌视。秦孝公死后贵族们诬告商鞅谋反。他逃到关口，想住旅舍，旅舍主人说："商鞅立的法律，如果收留没有证明的客人，就要连带受刑。"不肯接纳他，商鞅终于被杀害。

　　商鞅自己立的法律后来害了自己以致被杀。后世称之为作法自毙，并用以比喻自己定的办法害了自己。

Duke Xiao of Qin(秦孝公) employed Gongsun Yang (公孙鞅 390-338 B. C.) from the State of Wei (卫) as his prime minister. Gongsun Yang helped his master to reform the laws and change the backward customs of Qin, with the result that Qin became strong and prosperous. As a reward for his services he was given the fief of Shang(商), so he was called Shang Yang. But at the same time, he incurred the enmity of the Crown Prince and many nobles. After Duke Xiao of Qin died Shang Yang's enemies lodged a false accusation of treason against him, and Shang Yang was forced to flee. Intending to lodge at an inn near the border of the country, Shang Yang was rebuffed by the innkeeper, who said, "A law enacted by Shang Yang decrees punishment for an innkeeper who accepts a guest carrying no identification."

Forced to wander in the wilds, Shang Yang was finally captured and slain.

Thus Shang Yang was brought low by a law that he
himself had made. This was later called "making a law only
to fall foul of it oneself" to describe a situation in which a
man gets caught in his own trap or is hoist with his own
petard.

奇货可居

qí huò kě jū

A Rare Commodity Suitable for Hoarding

居:囤积。To store up, hoard for speculation.

战国时，秦国太子的儿子子楚作为人质被送到赵国国都邯郸①(Hándān)。由于秦国常常攻击赵国,子楚的处境很不好而且很穷。大商人吕不韦发现了子楚,十分高兴,他把子楚当作一件可以囤积的珍奇货物(奇货可居)。他把子楚请到自己的住处,告诉子楚他的父亲不久将继承王位,然后也要立太子。如果子楚能使他父亲的爱姬、没有儿子的华阳夫人认他为子,他就会被立为太子。(子楚的生母是一位不被他父亲宠爱的妃子。)经吕不韦积极活动,子楚逃回秦国,并被华阳夫人接受为子。不久子楚的父亲继承了王位,子楚被立为太子,一年后子楚的父亲死去,子楚继位为秦王。吕不韦则做了宰相,比从前更加富有。

后世用这个典故来比喻持某种特别条件或物品来谋取超常的利益。

In the Warring States Period, Zi Chu(子楚), the son of he crown prince of the State of Qin (秦), was sent to Iandan (邯郸), the capital of the State of Zhao (赵), as a ostage. As Qin attacked Zhao often, Zi Chu was in a very lifficult situation. A rich merchant, Lü Buwei, remarked hat Zi Chu was "a rare commodity suitable for hoarding." Ie invited Zi Chu to his house, and told him that his father vould succeed to the throne soon, and would make Zi Chu is crown prince so long as he could get his fater's favorite concubine, Madame Huayang （华阳夫人）, who had no son, to adopt him (Zi Chu's own mother was a neglected wife of his father). Lü Buwei then helped Zi Chu to escape back to Qin, where he was indeed adopted by Madame Huayang. Soon afterwards, his father succeeded to the throne, and Zi Chu was made his crown prince. A year later, when his father died, Zi Chu succeeded to the throne of Qin. He made Lü Buwei his prime minister.

Later, the allusion "a rare commodity suitable for hoarding" is used to describe seizing some special advantage or valuables to seek exorbitant profits.

注:① 邯郸:在今河北省邯郸市附近。
Near the present Handan City in Hebei （河北） Province.

逐客令

zhú kè lìng

Order for Guests to Leave

秦始皇(公元前 259—前 210)统一中国前,楚国人李斯(公元前?—前 208)来到秦国,成为客卿①。

后来韩国派了一个叫郑国的人到秦国劝秦王修灌溉渠,其目的是使秦国在修水渠的时候耗费大量人力物力,这样就没有力量去攻打韩国。秦王接受了郑国的建议修了郑国渠。后来秦王发现了韩国的企图,秦国的贵族就促使秦王下令驱逐所有由别国来的客卿,李斯也在驱逐之列。他上书给秦王说明这个做法不利于秦国的强大,于是秦王取消了这条逐客令。李斯留在秦国,后来当了丞相,帮助秦王统一了全国。

后世称要客人离去的要求为逐客令。

Before the First Emperor of Qin (秦始皇 259-210 B. C.) unified China, Li Si (李斯 ?-208 B. C.), a native of the State of Chu, went to the State of Qin (秦), where he was employed as a court official. Later, the State of Han (韩) sent a man named Zheng Guo (郑国) to Qin to persuade its ruler to build an irrigation canal. Han's real aim was to make Qin consume much manpower and resources in the project and render it incapable of invading Han. The ruler of Qin fell for this ruse, and built a canal called Zhengguo Canal. Later, Han's real intention was discovered and the advisers of the ruler urged him to expel all the foreign officials. Li Si was among those who were to be expelled. He sent a petition to the King, explaining that expelling all foreign officials would be disadvantageous to Qin. As a result, the ruler of Qin canceled the command. Li Si stayed in Qin, became the premier and subsequently helped it to conquer the whole country.

Later, the request for guests to leave came to be called "order for guests to leave".

注:① 客卿:秦官名。

　　Official title of Qin.

一字千金

yī zì qiān jīn

One Word Worth a Thousand Pieces of Gold

吕不韦当宰相后,广招门客①达三千之众。他为了扩大自己的名声并传之后世,命门客们将各自知道的事写出来,编在一起成书,名为《吕氏春秋》②。写成后又将书悬挂在秦国国都咸阳集市的门旁,上面挂了一千镒③(yì)黄金,写布告说,如果有人能将书中文章增、删一个字,就将这金子奖给他。由于人们惧怕吕不韦的权势,所以无人敢去改动。

后世用"一字千金"来赞扬某篇文章或文学作品写得好或重要。

When Lü Buwei became prime minister of the State of Qin (秦), he gathered around himself some 3,000 scholars. To extend his fame and hand it down to later generations, Lü Buwei ordered these retainers to write down everything they knew, and collected their writings in a book which he named *Lü's Annals*. When the book was completed, he had it hung on the gate of the market of Xianyang (咸阳), then the capital of Qin, together with 1,000 *yi* (镒) of gold and a notice saying that if anybody could justify adding or deleting one word in the book, he would be rewarded with the gold. As Lü Buwei was widely feared as a powerful man, nobody dared to claim the reward.

Later, the expression "one word worth a thousand pieces of gold," is used to praise well-written or very important piece of literature.

注:① 门客:官僚贵族招收和供养的有某种技能的人,为
　　 自己的政治活动服务。

　　 Men with all sorts of skills supported by aristocrats to
　　 aid them in their political activities.

② 《吕氏春秋》:"春秋"本为鲁国历史的名称,也成为
　　 那个历史阶段的名称,吕不韦用此名是为抬高他
　　 所编书的名声。

　　 Lü's Annals: Literally, *The Spring and Autumn* (春
　　 秋) *of Lü*. Spring and Autumn originally meant
　　 "chronology" and was first applied to the chronicles of
　　 the State. Lü Buwei used this name to heighten the
　　 prestige of his book.

③ 镒(yì):古代重量单位,合二十两。秦时称一镒为一
　　 金。

　　 An ancient unit of weight (= 20 *liang*). In the Qin
　　 Dynasty, one *yi* was one piece of gold.

燕雀焉知鸿鹄之志

yàn què yān zhī hónghú zhī zhì

How Can a Swallow Know the Aspirations of a Swan?

鸿鹄：天鹅。Swan.

　　陈胜 (公元前? —前 208) 年轻时和别人在一起做工。有一次,他停止耕作,站在地垄上懊丧了很久,对一起做工的人说:"如果谁今后得了富贵,不要互相忘记啊。"这些人笑他说:"你还在当雇工,怎么能得到富贵呢?"陈胜叹息说:"哎,燕雀怎么能知道鸿鹄的志向呢?(燕雀焉知鸿鹄之志)"后来陈胜发动反抗秦朝的起义,建立政权,被拥立为王。

　　后世以"燕雀焉知鸿鹄之志"来比喻庸碌之人不可能理解有伟大志向的人。

　　When Chen Sheng (陈胜 ?-208 B. C.) was young, he worked on the land as a hired hand. Once, he stopped ploughing and stood upon a ridge in a gloomy mood for a long time. Then he said to his fellow workers: "If any one of us becomes rich and famous in the future, let him not forget the others." His fellows laughed at him and said: "You are only a hired laborer; how can you become rich and famous?" Chen Sheng sighed: "Oh, how can a swallow know the aspirations of a swan?" Afterwards, Chen Sheng led an uprising against the rule of the Qin Dynasty and was made king.

　　Later, "How can a swallow know the aspirations of a swan" became used to comment on mediocre people who cannot understand people with great ambitions.

取而代之

qǔ ér dài zhī

Oust Him and Take His Place

公元前 210 年，也就是秦始皇在位的最后一年，他到会稽(Guìjī)①出巡，过浙江②。项羽(公元前232—前202)和他的叔父项梁一起去看秦始皇的仪仗。项羽看了以后说："可以除去他，占有他的地位(可取而代之)。"项梁赶快捂住他的嘴说："不要胡说，要满门被杀的呀！"但是项梁从此认为项羽是特别的人，而且项羽后来的确成为秦末农民起义军领袖。

后世用"取而代之"表示将他人赶走而自己占有其位置的行为。

In 210 B. C. the First Emperor of Qin (秦始皇) in the last year of his reign crossed the Zhe　(浙) River on an inspection tour to Guiji (会稽). Xiang Yu (项羽 232 B. C. - 202 B. C.) and his uncle Xiang Liang (项梁) went to watch the procession. Xiang Yu said,　"It is possible to oust him and take his place." Xiang Liang silenced him instantly, saying,　"Don't say such things,　or it will cost the lives of our whole family! " But from then on,　Xiang Liang regarded Xiang Yu as an outstanding person. In fact, Xiang Yu later became the leader of the rebel forces which overthrew the Qin Dynasty.

Later, this allusion became used to indicate the practice of shouldering aside another to take his position oneself.

注:① 会稽:今江苏省南部及浙江省大部。

In the southern part of modern Jiangsu (江苏) Province and part of Zhejiang (浙江) Province.

② 浙江:即钱塘江。

Also called the Qiantang (钱塘) River, is in modern Zhejiang (浙江) Province.

先发制人

xiān fā zhì rén

Gain the Initiative by Striking First

公元前 209 年,各地都有人起兵反秦。会稽的郡(jùn)守①来找项梁说:"先下手就能控制别人(先发制人),后动手就要被人控制,我想请你和我一起立即起兵。"项梁假装同意,叫来他的侄子项羽,示意项羽杀掉郡守。项羽杀掉了郡守和他手下一百多人,这样会稽一带的人便都拥项梁为首领起兵反秦。

后世以"先发制人"来说明先动手就可制服别人。

In 209 B. C. revolts against the Qin Dynasty were raging everywhere. The magistrate of Guiji (会稽) went to see Xiang Liang and said, "He who strikes first will gain the initiative, while he who delays will be subjugated. So I have come to ask you to join me in revolt at once." Xiang Liang pretented to agree. He then instigated his nephew Xiang Yu to slay the the magistrate and his more than 100 followers. Thereupon, the people of the Guiji area flocked to Xiang Liang and followed him in the struggle to topple the Qin Dynasty.

Later, "gain the initiative by striking first" is used to mean that he who acted first would subdue the others.

注:① 郡守: 郡是古代的行政区划, 比县小; 秦汉以后比
　　　县大。郡守就是郡的首领。

　　　Jun refers to prefectures in ancient times, which were
　　　smaller than counties before the Qin and Han dynas-
　　　ties and bigger after that. Junshou is the head of the
　　　prefecture.

一败涂地

yī bài tú dì

A Defeat That Brings Everything Crashing Down

公元前 209 年，秦二世登基，秦朝已衰败，各地都发生反秦起义。后来成为汉朝皇帝的刘邦（公元前 256—前 195），那时已聚集了萧何、曹参、周勃、樊哙（Kuài）等一百多人，他写信给沛县人说："全国人都反对秦朝，各地都在起义，只有起义才可以保存家室。"于是沛县人杀掉县官，开城门迎接刘邦，要求他做新县令。刘邦说："如果选择的人不合适就会失败而丧失一切（一败涂地），我的能力不足，请另选别人。"但是大家认为刘邦最好，于是推举他为县令。

后世用"一败涂地"这句话来表示完全失败。

In 209 B. C. the second emperor of the Qin Dynasty (秦二世) ascended the throne. The dynasty was in decline, and the whole country was in revolt. Liu Bang (256-195 B. C.), later the founder of the Han Dynasty, had gathered more than a hundred men around him. He sent a message to the citizens of Pei county, saying, "All the nation is against the rule of Qin, and uprisings are taking place everywhere. Only revolt can save you now. " So the people of Pei killed their magistrate and opened the city gate to Liu Bang, whom they wanted to elect as their magistrate. Liu Bang told them: "If the man chosen is not suitable, you will be defeated, and that will bring everything crashing down. I do not have sufficient ability, so please elect somebody else. " But the people thought Liu Bang was the most suitable person for the job, and made him Lord of Pei.

Later, "a defeat that brings everything crashing down" came to be used to describe a crushing and complete failure.

孺子可教

rúzǐ kě jiào

The Child Is Worth Instructing

孺子:小孩子。 Child.

张良 (公元前?—前 186) 年轻时,一次在下邳 (pī) ①的一座桥上散步,见一个老人把鞋掉到桥下,老人对张良说:"年轻人,下去把鞋捡上来。"张良很感意外,想揍这老人,但看他年老,就忍住气,下桥把鞋捡上来。老人又伸出脚说:"给我穿上"。张良就跪下给他穿上。老人笑着走了,又回头对张良说:"你这个年轻人可以教导 (孺子可教矣),五天后的黎明到这里来见我。"

以后张良去了两次,但是老人都已先到,还指责张良迟到。最后张良半夜就去,过一会老人也到了,对张良说:"应当这样。"他给张良一本书说:"读了这本书,可以做帝王的教师。"张良拿回去研读,这本书是《太公②兵法》。以后张良辅佐刘邦建立了汉朝,被封为留侯。

后世以"孺子可教"来形容有培养前途的青年人。

Once, when he was very young, Zhang Liang (张良 ? -186 B. C.) was strolling across a bridge in Xiapi. He saw an old man drop his shoe from the bridge. The old man said to Zhang Liang: "Young fellow, go and fetch my shoe." Zhang Liang was astonished, and wanted to strike the old man, but he restrained himself because of the other's advanced age. So he fetched the shoe. The old man stretched out his foot and said, "Put it on for me! " Zhang Liang knelt down and did so. The old man walked away, laughing, but turned his head and said, "Young fellow, you are worth instructing. Meet me here at dawn in five days' time." After that, Zhang Liang went there twice, but the old man was already there, and reproved him for being late. Then Zhang Liang went to the bridge at midnight. The old man arrived late, and said, "That's how it ought to be." He gave a book to Zhang Liang, saying, "Read this, and you will become the instructor of kings and emperors." Zhang Liang took the book — *The Art of War of the Grand Elder*. Afterwards, he assisted Liu Bang to establish the Han Dynasty and was made Duke of Liu (留).

Later, "The child is worth instructing" came to be used to describe promising young men.

注:① 下邳:在今江苏省邳县南。

Located in the south of the present Pi County (邳) in present-day Jiangsu Province.

② 太公:指周朝姜太公,即姜尚。

The Grand Elder refers to Grand Elder Jiang of the Zhou (周) Dynasty, i. e. Jiang Shang (姜尚).

壁上观

bì shàng guān

Watching the Battle From the Ramparts

项羽的军队和秦军在巨鹿①大战的时候，各路起义军也陆续到达。但是他们都怕秦军而不敢出战，只站在营寨的围墙上看（"诸将皆从壁上观"）。项羽的军队人数只有秦军的二十分之一，但是个个奋勇战斗，呼声动地，其他军队看着都感到恐怖。最后项羽的军队消灭了秦军，取得完全的胜利。各路将领去见项羽时，都低着头不敢仰视。以后项羽就统帅了各路起义军。

后世用"壁上观"比喻在别人发生冲突时自己不参与只是旁观的作法。

When the rebel army of Xiang Yu （项羽） was fighting the forces of the Qin （秦） emperor at Julu （巨鹿①） in 211 B. C. bands of other rebel troops arrived. But they feared the Qin army, and dared not join Xiang Yu. They simply stood on the ramparts of their fortifications and watched the fighting. Xiang Yu's men were outnumbered 20 to one, but they fought bravely, their war cries shaking the very earth. Those who were watching were awe-struck. At last, the Qin army was crushed, and Xiang Yu emerged as the most powerful man in the empire. When the other rebel generals visited Xiang Yu they bowed their heads and dared not look up at him. Afterwards, Xiang Yu took command of all the anti-Qin armies.

Later, "watching the battle from the ramparts" came to be used to denote the attitude of being an onlooker but not a participant in other people's conflicts.

注:① 巨鹿:在今河北省平乡县西南。

Located in the southwest part of present-day Pingxiang （平乡） County in Hebei （河北） Province.

成也萧何，败也萧何

chéng yě Xiāo Hé, bài yě Xiāo Hé

Raised Up by Xiao He and Cast Down by Xiao He

韩信（公元前？—前196）原来在项羽的军队中担任低级军官，不被重视，于是他离开项羽到刘邦的军中，仍不被重视。刘邦的主要谋士之一萧何（公元前？—前193）与韩信谈了几次话，认为韩信是奇才，就推荐给刘邦，但是刘邦还是不重视他，韩信因此逃跑了。萧何听说之后，连夜去把他追了回来，并且告诉刘邦说如果想得天下就必须任用韩信统帅军队。刘邦看见萧何如此重视韩信，就改变了态度，在隆重的仪式上任命韩信为大将军。在以后打败项羽和统一中原的战争中，韩信屡战屡胜，为建立汉朝立了大功。但是刘邦总怕韩信谋反，因而屡次降低他的职位，并把他留在首都。到公元前196年，韩信与分封在外的将军合谋造反。当时刘邦在外征讨，萧何与吕后一起设计将韩信骗入皇宫，将他逮捕处死。这样韩信的被起用和被杀都是由萧何安排的。

后世用"成也萧何，败也萧何"这句话来说某人、某事的成功与失败都是由一人造成的。

Han Xin (韩信 ?-196 B. C.) was a junior officer in the army of Xiang Yu. Passed over for promotion, he left to join the army of Xiang Yu's rival Liu Bang. Again, despite being recommended by Xiao He, one of Liu Bang's chief advisors, Han Xin failed to gain promotion. So he deserted. When Xiao He learned of this he had him pursued and brought back. Xiao He told Liu Bang that if he wanted to conquer the entire country he must entrust command of the army to Han Xin. When Liu Bang realized that Xiao He valued Han Xin so highly, he changed his attitude and appointed Han Xin his supreme commander in a solemn ceremony. In the following battles against Xiang Yu and to unify the country, Han Xin won victory after victory, and rendered very meritorious service in establishing the Han Dynasty. Afterwards, Liu Bang feared that Han Xin might stage a coup against him, so he demoted him several times, but kept him in the capital.

In 196 B. C. Han Xin conspired with another general when Liu Bang was away campaigning. Xiao He plotted with the Empress Lü Zhi （吕雉）to entice Han Xin to go to the palace. There he was arrested and executed. Thus both the elevation and destruction of Han Xin were arranged by Xiao He.

The saying "raised up by Xiao He and cast down by Xiao He" is used to indicate success and failure both caused by the same person.

逐鹿中原

zhú lù zhōngyuán

Hunting Deer in the Central Plains

鹿：猎取的对象，喻称政权。 Deer, prey, i. e. regime, throne, state power.

中原：黄河中下游地区，泛指中国。 Central Plains in the area of the middle and lower reaches of the Yellow River — in those days "China Proper".

公元前 203 年，韩信被封为齐王，他的谋士蒯（Kuǎi）通劝韩信脱离刘邦。但是韩信没有接受他的意见。到公元前 196 年，韩信以谋反罪被杀。皇帝刘邦听说蒯通曾劝韩信造反，就把他捕到京城要处死他。蒯通说："秦朝失掉了他的鹿，天下人都来追逐，只有能力强，跑得快的人可以抓到它。一家的狗向别人叫并不是因为别家的人坏，而只是因为那不是他的主人。我那时只知为韩信谋划，不认识陛下，所以处死我是冤枉的。"刘邦听后就赦免了蒯通。

后世用"逐鹿中原"这句话来比喻争夺政权，或者再加上一句"未知鹿死谁手"来说明争夺的结果尚未可知。

In 203 B. C. Han Xin (韩信) was made King of Qi (齐) by the first Han Dynasty emperor, Liu Bang. His adviser Kuai Tong (蒯通) urged him to break away from Liu Bang and divide the empire together with the kings of Han and Chu, but Han Xin did not accept his suggestion. In 196 B. C. Han Xin was executed for plotting a rebellion. Liu Bang heard that Kuai Tong had urged Han Xin to rebel, so he had Kuai Tong arrested and brought to the capital to be executed. Kuai Tong said to Liu Bang: "When the Qin Dynasty lost its deer, everybody in the country joined in the hunt for it, but only the able and swift had a chance to catch it. A dog barks at other people, not because they are bad but because they are not its master. At that time I knew only that my duty was to help Han Xin to gain power; I did not know Your Majesty. So executing me would be unjust." Thereupon, Liu Bang pardoned him.

Later, the metaphor "hunting deer in the central plains" came to be used to describe a struggle for power. Another version is "at whose hand the deer will die is unknown" meaning that the outcome of a struggle or rivalry is still uncertain.

约法三章

yuē fǎ sān zhāng

Agreeing on a Three-Point Law

公元前 206 年,秦王子婴向刘邦投降,刘邦首先进入秦都咸阳①。刘邦看到秦宫奢(shē)华,里面有许多宝物和美女,就想住在秦宫中。樊哙和张良劝他不要图安乐而失去民心。于是刘邦回到军队中住。他邀请当地领袖和老人们来见面,对他们说:"大家长久被秦朝苛刻的法律所苦。我将要在关中②为王,现在和大家约定三条法律:杀人要处死,伤害别人和盗窃的要定罪,其他的秦朝法律都废除。"然后又命令秦国的地方官吏通告各处。于是秦人都拥护刘邦。

后世用"约法三章"来表示简单明确的规定。

In 206 B. C. Zi Ying (子婴), emperor of the Qin (秦) Dynasty, surrendered to Liu Bang. When the latter entered Xianyang (咸阳), the capital of Qin, he saw that the imperial palace was a splendid edifice filled with treasures and beautiful women. Naturally, he wanted to stay there, but his advisors Zhang Liang and Fan Kuai persuaded him not to wallow in enjoyment and luxury, otherwise he would lose the loyalty of his people. So Liu Bang went back to stay with his army. He summoned the local leaders and elders to him, and said to them: "You all suffered for a long time under the tyranny of Qin. Now I am to rule Guanzhong. I now decree a three-point law: Those who kill shall be executed; those who cause injury shall be punished; and those who steal and rob shall be convicted. All other laws of Qin are abolished."

Then the local officials were ordered to spread knowledge of the new law. This was how Liu Bang won the allegiance of the people of Qin.

Later, the phrase "agreeing on a three-point law" came to be used to describe concise and explicit law or rule.

注：① 秦都咸阳在今陕西省咸阳市东北。

Capital of the Qin（秦）Dynasty. It was located northeast of present-day Xianyang City in Shaanxi（陕西）Province.

② 关中在今陕西省中部，西安市东西各二百公里内的地方。

In the central part of Shaanxi, less than 200 km from modern Xi'an City.

鸿门宴
Hóngmén yàn

项庄舞剑，意在沛公
Xiàng Zhuāng wǔ jiàn, yì zài Pèigōng

The Banquet and Sword Dance at Hongmen

刘邦攻下关中以后，他的军队有十万人，驻于灞（Bà）上①。不久项羽也进入关中，带兵四十万，驻于鸿门②，两军相距四十里。项羽听了别人的挑拨，准备进攻刘邦。项羽的叔父项伯与刘邦的谋士张良是好朋友，他夜里到刘邦的军营叫张良赶快逃跑。张良认为这时逃跑是不对的，于是引项伯去见刘邦。刘邦款待了项伯并和他订了儿女亲事。刘邦向他说自己并无与项羽为敌之意。项伯答应替刘邦在项羽面前说好话，又当夜回到自己的军营向项羽转告了刘邦的话，要求项羽善待刘邦，项羽答应了这个要求。

第二天，刘邦带了张良、樊哙等一百多人来到鸿门，当面向项羽解释。项羽设宴招待刘邦。在宴会上，项羽的谋士范增三次示意项羽杀掉刘邦，但是项羽不予理会。于是范增叫来项庄，叫他进帐祝寿，然后在席上舞剑，乘机杀死刘邦。在项庄舞剑时，项伯也拔剑起舞，常以身体掩护刘邦使项庄不能下手。这时张良叫大力士樊哙冲进举行宴会的帐房，使项庄停止舞剑，樊哙还批评项羽要杀有功之人。

刘邦假装出去上厕所，乘机带着樊哙等四个人逃回了自己的军营。

后世以"鸿门宴"来比喻一方对另一方施以要挟（yāoxié）③、威胁行为的宴会。以"项庄舞剑，意在沛公"来比喻暗中别有意图的行为。

When Liu Bang entered the Guanzhong area of pre-sent-day Shannxi Province, he stationed his army of 100,000 men at Bashang (灞上). He found himself facing Xiang Yu's forces numbering 400,000 stationed at Hongmen (鸿门), only some 40 *li* away.

As Xiang Yu was preparing for an all-out attack on his rival, his uncle, Xiang Bo (项伯), sneaked into the camp of Liu Bang to warn his friend Zhang Liang, who was Liu Bang's chief advisor, that he had better flee. However, Zhang Liang refused to do so, and, instead, introduced Xiang Bo to his master. Liu Bang was delighted to meet Xiang Bo and asked him to arrange peace between himself and Xiang Yu. He even went so far as to arrange a marriage between his and Xiang Bo's children.

The next day Liu Bang went to Hongmen, accompanied by Zhang Liang and only 100 horsemen. At a banquet that evening, Fan Zeng (范增), the chief advisor to Xiang Yu, secretly urged his lord three times to take advantage of the occasion to kill Liu Bang, but all in vain. Thereupon, Fan Zeng summoned Xiang Zhuang (项庄) and instructed him to perform a sword dance, during which he should look out for a chance to slay Liu Bang. But when this man started his sword dance, Xiang Bo, who suspected treachery, drew his own sword and danced along with him, thus effectively shielding Liu Bang from harm.

Later, Liu Bang made an excuse to leave the banquet, and escaped.

Later, the phrase "banquet at Hongmen" came to be used to mean an entertainment laid on to threaten or coerce the guest of honor. "Xiang Zhuang's sword dance" means something similar. Both expressions refer to seemingly friendly acts with hostile intent.

注:① 灞上:在今陕西省西安市东。

East of modern Xi'an City in Shaanxi (陕西) Province.

② 鸿门:在今陕西省临潼县东。

East of the present-day Lintong County in Shaanxi Province.

③ 要挟:利用对方的弱点,强迫对方答应自己的要求。

A Chinese measure of distance. Forty *li* was about 20 km.

人为刀俎，我为鱼肉

rén wéi dāo zǔ,　wǒ wéi yú ròu

They Are the Knife and Chopping Block, While We Are the Fish and Meat

俎：古代割肉类用的砧（zhēn）板。　Meat chopping block in ancient China.

在鸿门宴上，刘邦借去厕所出了帐房，接着把樊哙也叫了出去。项羽这时派人去叫刘邦回帐房。刘邦却想借这个机会逃走，他对樊哙说："我出来的时候没有辞行，现在怎么办呢？"樊哙说："重要的行动中不能顾小节，为了大事不能顾小的失礼。现在人家是刀和砧板，我们是鱼和肉（人为刀俎，我为鱼肉），还辞行做什么？"于是刘邦带了樊哙等四个人立即走小路回到了自己的军营。

后世用"人为刀俎，我为鱼肉"来形容生死掌握在别人手里，自己处在任人宰割的境地。

At the Hongmen banquet, when Liu Bang left the tent, having been alerted to the plot against his life, he took his aide Fan Kuai (樊哙) with him. He said to the latter, "I did not take leave of my host. I must escape, but how can I simply depart so rudely?" Fan Kuai said, "A great cause should not be hampered by details or petty points of etiquette. Xiang Yu and his advisors are the knife and the chopping block, while we are the fish and the meat. So why stand on ceremony?" So Liu Bang left at once, together with Fan Kuai and three other men, making his way back to his own camp on foot.

Later, "They are the knife and the chopping block, while we are the fish and the meat" came to be used to describe the situation of being at the mercy of others.

明修栈道，暗度陈仓

míng xiū zhàndào, àn dù Chéncāng

Repairing the Road While Making a Secret Detour

公元前 205 年，刘邦被立为汉王。由于项羽军事势力强大，刘邦不得不带三万人回封地汉中①。汉中被大山阻隔，进入汉中要走栈道。栈道是在悬崖峭壁上打孔，插进木架，木架上铺木板做成的通道。刘邦的队伍通过以后就放火烧了栈道，向项羽表示没有回来的意图。过了大约半年，刘邦派人修复栈道，迷惑了项羽的军队。他们以为要等栈道修好，刘邦才会向关中进军，而刘邦的大军却暗中翻山从陈仓②隘（ài）道③进入了关中，使项羽守军措手不及并被打败。刘邦就这样开始与项羽争夺中原。

后世用"明修栈道，暗度陈仓"来比喻某些人以表面上的某种动作为掩护，而秘密使用其他方法达到目的。

In 205 B. C. Liu Bang was crowned King of Han. But as the military strength of his arch-rival, Xiang Yu was much stronger, Liu Bang was forced to retreat with his 30,000 men to his stronghold of Hanzhong. This area was surrounded by mountains, and the main way to approach it was along a plank road built on the face of a cliff. Liu Bang burned the plank road as soon as his men were safely past it to show Xiang Yu that he had no intention of returning and to prevent pursuit. After about half a year, Liu Bang sent men to rebuild the road, so naturally Xiang Yu thought that an attack was being prepared along that route, and that it would not be forthcoming until the road had been made serviceable again. But meanwhile Liu Bang secretly led a force into Guanzhong by way of the perilous Chencang Pass and caught Xiang Yu by surprise. From then on, Liu Bang began to contend with Xiang Yu for the central parts of China.

Later, "repairing the road while making a secret detour" came to be used to describe an obvious action which is camouflage for a devious stratagem.

注：① 汉中：在今陕西省西南部汉中地区。

　　In the southwest part of modern Shaanxi Province.

② 陈仓：古县名，在今陕西省西部宝鸡市东，是汉中、关中两地区之间的必经之地。

　　East of present-day Baoji City in the western part of Shaanxi Province. It is the main pass linking the Hanzhong and Guanzhong regions.

③ 隘道：狭窄、险要的道路。

　　Defile.

背水一战

bèi shuǐ yī zhàn

Fighting With One's Back to the River

公元前 205 年，韩信带汉兵在现在的河北省西部进攻赵国①。他先在赵军附近埋伏了一支军队，然后将大部分军队背着河对着赵军列阵。赵军都大笑，认为他们不懂兵法。交战时，赵军全部出动来捉韩信，韩信退入河边的汉军中，这些汉军因无退路而不得不拼死作战。赵军不能取胜就退回自己的营寨，但汉军伏兵已占领了营寨，赵军于是大乱，汉军两面夹击，赵军大败，主将被杀，赵王被俘虏。在庆祝胜利时汉军将领问韩信，背水列阵不合兵法，而这次竟然取胜是什么道理。韩信说兵法里有"置之死地而后生"。汉军的士兵多是由别的军队投降过来的，把他们放在没有退路的地方自然要拼死而战，如果将他们放在有退路的地方，他们遇敌就会逃跑，无法统帅了。

后世用"背水一战"来比喻没有退路的决一死战。

In 205 B. C. Han Xin led an imperial army of the Han Dynasty against the upstart Kingdom of Zhao, in the western part of modern Hebei Province（河北省）. First, he sent troops to lay an ambush near the camp of the Zhao army. Then he ordered the major part of his army to line up facing the Zhao camp and with a river behind them. The soldiers of Zhao laughed at him for this tactical mistake. But, with no way to retreat, the imperial troops had no choice but to fight desperately, and they beat off the Zhao troops. When the Zhao soldiers retreated to their camp, they found that it had been taken by the ambushers. As a result of being caught in a pincer movement, the Zhao army was crushed, its commander slain, and the King of Zhao captured. At the victory banquet, his subordinates asked Han Xin why he had lined his men up with a river behind them, as this was against the arts of war. Han Xin said, "In such a situation, man will fight because it is impossible to flee. Our soldiers are mostly from other armies that surrendered. Put them in a place with no way to retreat, then they will naturally fight desperately. If they were put in a place from which it was possible to retreat, they would do so. "

Later, the metaphor "fighting with one's back to the river" came to be used to describe making do-or-die efforts.

注：① 赵国：秦亡后由起义者建立的国家。

The Kingdom of Zhao was established by uprisers at the fall of the Qin Dynasty.

匹夫之勇　妇人之仁

pǐfū zhī yǒng　fùrén zhī rén

Reckless Courage and Feminine Benevolence

　　韩信被拜为大将军后,他对刘邦说:我曾是项羽的部下,请让我评论他。当项羽发威的时候,所有的人都会害怕后退,但是他不能任用有能力的将军,他只有匹夫之勇。他对人恭敬仁慈,态度和蔼,有人生病时,他会流着眼泪将自己的食物分给他们。但是有人立了功应当封爵(jué)的时候,官印刻好了,他却拿在手里不愿意给人,这就是妇人之仁。韩信最后的结论是项羽是可以被打败的。

　　后世以"匹夫之勇","妇人之仁"来形容无助于成就大事、达到主要目标的勇敢与仁慈。

After Han Xin was appointed commander-in-chief, he said to Liu Bang, "I used to serve Xiang Yu, so please let me tell you what kind of a man he is. When Xiang Yu manifests his majesty, all men shrink in dread. But he is loath to delegate authority to able generals. He has only the braveness of a reckless man. He is respectful, kind and amiable by nature. If someone falls ill, he will weep and send them tasty morsels. But when somebody renders meritorious service that ought to be rewarded with titles and fe-offs, he grasps the seals of office tightly, unwilling to let slip any of his power. This is the so-called feminine benevolence." The conclusion of Han Xin was that Xiang Yu could be defeated by taking advantage of his weaknesses.

Later, the phrase "reckless courage and feminine benevolence" came to be used to describe the types of braveness and kindness that do not help to obtain the main object of an activity.

养虎遗患

yǎng hǔ yí huàn

To Rear a Tiger Is to Court Calamity

公元前 202 年，刘邦的汉国和项羽的楚国连年战争，相持日久，双方都处在困苦之中。这时两军在黄河南岸荥(xíng)阳①一带对峙(zhì)②。楚军战斗力强，但缺乏粮食，汉军战斗力不如楚军，但粮食充裕。刘邦派人去说服了项羽，两家相约中分天下，以鸿沟为界，东边归楚、西边归汉。项羽将以前俘虏的刘邦的父亲、妻子、儿女归还，然后领兵东归，士兵都很高兴。刘邦也准备西撤。张良、陈平劝他说："楚兵现在已经疲乏，又无粮食，应当乘此机会消灭楚军，如果不这样做就是所谓'养虎自遗患'。"于是刘邦聚集军队追击项羽，最后消灭了楚军，项羽自杀。

后世以"养虎遗患"来比喻留下敌人给自己造成祸害、危险。

In 202 B. C. the army of Han, led by Liu Bang, had been at war for years with the army of Chu, led by Xiang Yu. Both sides were wearied with the hardships of continuous campaigning. By then they were pitted against each other in the area of Xingyang. The Chu army had high morale but was short of food, while the Han army was weaker but had abundant food. Liu Bang sent envoys to persuade Xiang Yu that they should divide the country between them, with Honggou as the boundary — east of Honggou would belong to Chu, and west of it would belong to Han. Xiang Yu returned Liu Bang's captured father, wife and children, and then retreated eastward, to the great relief of his men. Liu Bang was also preparing to retreat, but his advisers Zhang Liang (张良) and Chen Ping (陈平) said to him, "Now the Chu army is exhausted and lacking in food, we ought to seize the opportunity and wipe them out. If we do not do so, it will be like the saying 'to rear a tiger is to court calamity'. " So Liu Bang rallied his forces and pursued the Chu army, finally wiping them out. Thereupon Xiang Yu killed himself.

Later, the saying "To rear a tiger is to court calamity" came to be used to indicate that appeasement brings disaster.

注:① 荥阳:在今河南省荥阳市附近。

Located near the present Xingyang City in Henan Province.

② 对峙:两方面相持不下。

To be at a stalemate; stand opposite each other.

衣锦夜行

yī jǐn yè xíng

Walking at Night in Silken Robes

在鸿门宴会之后不久，项羽带兵攻进咸阳城，杀了秦降王子婴，烧毁了秦朝宫殿，劫掠了财富和宫女向东回归。有人对项羽说："关中四面有山河保护，土地肥沃，在这里建都可以控制全国。"但是项羽看到秦朝宫殿都已毁坏，又怀念家乡，于是他说："有了富贵不回故乡，就像身穿锦绣衣裳晚上走路，有谁能知道呢！"因此决心东归。

后世用"衣锦夜行"来比喻不能使人看到自己的荣誉、富贵。

Soon after the Hongmen banquet, Xiang Yu led his army to capture Xianyang（咸阳）. He killed Ziying, the surrendered king of Qin, burned the palaces of Qin and began to retreat eastwards with looted treasures and kidnapped women. One of his advisors urged him to stay in the Guanzhong area, saying, "Guanzhong is protected on all sides by mountains and rivers, and the land is fertile. Establish your capital here, and then you will be able to control the whole country."

But Xiang Yu saw the palaces of Qin had been destroyed, and he was homesick. He said, "Not returning to one's native land after getting rich and holding high office is like walking at night in silken robes. Who would know of your good fortune?" So he was determined to return eastwards.

Later, this metaphor "walking at night in silken robes"

came to refer to not being able to show one's wealth and rank
to the public.

沐猴而冠

mùhóu ér guàn

A Monkey With a Hat on

沐猴：猕（mí）猴。　Rhesus monkey.

冠：戴上帽子。　To wear a hat.

项羽决定衣锦还乡之后，劝他在关中建都立业的人在背后嘲笑说："人家说楚国人是'猕猴戴帽子'，的确如此。"项羽听说这话，就把那个人处死了。

后世用"沐猴而冠"或"沐猴而冠带"的话讽刺那些目光短浅、徒（tú）①有仪表，不能成大事的人。

When Xiang Yu decided to return home after capturing the capital of the Qin Dynasty, the advisor who had urged him to establish his capital in Guanzhong (关中) ridiculed him behind his back, saying, "The natives of the State of Chu (楚) are said to be nothing more than monkeys wearing hats. I have found that this really is the case." When Xiang Yu heard about this, he had the man executed.

Later, the phrase "a monkey with a hat on" or "a monkey wearing hats and ribbons" came to be used to mock short-sighted and worthless people who are dressed up in imposing attire.

注:① 徒:"仅仅"的意思，表示除此以外没有别的。
　　 Only.

韩信将兵，多多益善

Hán Xìn jiàng bīng, duō duō yì shàn

The More Troops Han Xin Commands, the Better

将：带（兵）。 To command (troops).

刘邦当了皇帝以后，和韩信评论各将领的能力。刘邦问韩信："像我这样能领多少兵？"韩信回答说："陛（bì）下①不过能领十万兵。"刘邦又问："那么你怎样呢？"韩信说："我领的兵越多越好（'多多益善'）。"刘邦笑了起来说："越多越好吗？那你怎么成了我的属下呢？"韩信说："陛下不善于领兵，但善于统帅将领，这就是我成为陛下下属的原因。"刘邦听了哈哈大笑。

后世用这个比喻时，常常只用后半句，意思是说某些人或某些东西越多越好。

Soon after Liu Bang became emperor of Han, he discussed the abilities of his generals with Han Xin. He asked, "How many soldiers could a person like myself command?" Han Xin answered, "Your Majesty could command only 100, 000. " Liu Bang asked again, "Then how about you?" Han Xin answered, "In my case, the more the better. " Liu Bang laughed, and said, "If that is so, then why are you my subject?" Han Xin answered, "Your Majesty's talent does not lie in commanding troops but in commanding generals. That is why I am your Majesty's subject. " Liu Bang laughed heartily at this.

Later, this expression came to mean "the more the better. "

注:① 陛下:对君主的尊称。
Your Majesty.

无面目见江东①父老

wú miànmù jiàn jiāng dōng fùlǎo

Too Ashamed to Face the Elders East of the Yangtze

公元前 202 年,项羽的军队在垓下 (Gāixià) ②被汉军围困,他在夜里带了八百多人突围,汉军不断追击,最后项羽只剩下二十六人。他们到了乌江③准备过长江东去。乌江亭长准备了一条船要求他赶快渡江, 项羽说:"我带了江东八千子弟过江西去,现在没有一人回来,我有什么面目去见江东父老呢?"于是反身冲入汉军之中,杀了数百人,自己也负伤十几处,最后自刎(wěn)④而死。

后世用"无面目见江东父老"来形容遭到重大失败之后不好意思见故乡的父老乡亲。

In 202 B. C. Xiang Yu and his army were besieged by the Han army at Gaixia (垓下). One night he broke out of the encirclement with only about 800 men. The Han army continued to pursue him, until he had only 26 men left. When they reached a village called Wujiang (乌江), intending to cross the Yangtze River to the east, the head of the village prepared a boat for Xiang Yu, and urged him to cross at once. Xiang Yu said, "When I crossed the River and went west, I took with me 8,000 sons and brothers from east of the Yangtze. Now none of them has returned; how can I face the elders east of the Yangtze?" Then he turned and attacked the Han army, killed hundreds of the enemy, and suffered many wounds himself. Finally, he cut his own throat and perished.

Later, the expression, "too ashamed to face the elders

east of the Yangtze" came to be used to describe the feelings of a person who is too ashamed to face the people back home after failing miserably at some venture.

注:① 江东:长江在安徽东部由西南走向东北,今江苏南部在长江之东。那是项羽起兵之处。

East of the Yangtze: in the eastern part of modern Anhui Province （安徽省）, the Yangtze River flows from southwest to northeast. So the southern part of Jiangsu Province （江苏省） is east of the river, and that was the place where Xiang Yu started his campaign.

② 垓下:在今安徽省灵璧县东南。

Located in the southeast of present-day Lingbi County （灵璧县） in Anhui Province （安徽省）.

③ 乌江:在今安徽省和县东北,此处已近长江。

Located in the northeast of present-day He County （和县） in Anhui Province, near the Yangtze.

④ 刎:用刀割脖子。

Cut one's throat.

运筹帷幄

yùn chóu wéiwò

Manipulating Victory From the Command Tent

筹:计策。 Strategy.

帷幄:古时军中帐幕。 Command tent in ancient China.

本篇题目来源于刘邦对张良的评论。公元前202年，刘邦在洛阳问群臣为什么他能得天下，为什么项羽会失败。他认为坐在帐幕中策划，使千里之外的战争获胜，自己不如张良；使国家安定，安抚百姓，供给军饷，自己不如萧何；带领百万军队，每战必胜，凡攻必克，自己不如韩信。这三个人都是杰出的人，能够重用他们所以才得天下。项羽只有一个范增，还不能用他的计策，所以要失败。

后世用"运筹帷幄"表示在军帐内谋划，指挥前方作战。也泛指善于筹划，指挥全局。

This is a story about Liu Bang's appraisal of his generals.

One day in 202 B. C. Liu Bang, having gained the imperial, was sitting in his capital Luoyang and discussing with his officials why he had been able to win the empire, and why Xiang Yu had failed to do so. He admitted that he was inferior to Zhang Liang when it came to sitting in the command tent and devising a victorious strategy for a battle one thousand *li* away. "Moreover," he said, "I am not as good as Xiao He when it comes to pacifying the country, making the common people content and furnishing provisions for the army." Furthermore, he admitted to being no match for Han Xin when it came to leading an army of a million men and achieving victory in every battle.

"But," he pointed out, "I recognized the outstanding

qualities of these men, and was shrewd enough to place them in important positions. Xiang Yu, on the other hand, had only one excellent adviser, and that was Fan Zeng. But he did not even heed the advice of Fan Zeng! That was why he lost the empire and I gained it."

Later, "manipulating victory from the command tent" came to be used to praise someone who is good at controlling a tricky situation.

狡兔死，走狗烹

jiǎo tù sǐ, zǒu gǒu pēng

When the Crafty Hares Have Been Exterminated, the Hunting Dogs Will Be Cooked

此语原出《韩非子》①。

公元 201 年，韩信为楚王，有人告他谋反，刘邦以巡游云梦泽②为名到了楚国③，乘韩信来朝见时将他逮捕。韩信说："果然如别人所说：'狡猾的兔子死了，优良的猎狗就要被煮了吃；高飞的鸟消失了，好的弓就要被收起来；敌对的国家灭亡了，谋士就得死。'现在天下平定了，我就该被杀。"这一次刘邦放了韩信，封他为淮阴④侯。

这些话在后世减缩为"狡兔死，走狗烹"，意思是说事情办成功，有功之臣就要被杀害。

This saying originated in the book *Han Fei Zi* （韩非子）.

In 201 B. C. Han Xin, King of Chu （楚） was suspected by emperor Liu Bang of plotting a rebellion. The emperor accordingly went to his domain on the pretex of inspecting the Yunmeng （云梦） Marshes and had Han Xin arrested when he came to pay homage. Han Xin said, "As the saying goes, 'When the crafty hares have been exterminated, the hunting dogs will be cooked; when the partridges are extinguished, the fine bows will be put away; when all enemies are conquered, the advisors will be killed. ' Now the empire is at peace, so I ought to be killed. " Liu Bang, however, absolved him of blame, and enfeoffed him as the Duke of Huaiyin （淮阴）.

Later, the saying "When the crafty hares are extermi-

nated, the hunting dogs will be cooked" came to be used to
mean that when a scheme succeeds those who made its success possible are no longer needed or even killed.

注:① 《韩非子》:是集韩非(约公元前 280—前 233) 著作
　　　和他人论述韩非学说文章的文集，内容是治国的
　　　方法。
　　　Han Fei Zi: a collection of the sayings of Han Fei
　　　(韩非 280-233 B. C.) and comments on them. The
　　　contents center on ways to rule a state.

　② 云梦泽:在今湖南、湖北西部，长江南北的古代沼
　　　泽,现已消失。
　　　Yunmeng Marshes: an ancient marshland located in
　　　the western parts of Hubei and Hunan （湖 南）
　　　provinces, on both sides of the Yangzi (杨子) River,
　　　now dried up.

　③ 楚国:为汉朝所建,在今江苏到湖北一带。
　　　The Kingdom of Chu: established by the Han
　　　Dynasty, it was situated in the area of present-day
　　　Hubei (湖北) to Jiangsu (江苏) provinces.

　④ 淮阴:在江苏省北部,是韩信的故乡。但韩信被封
　　　后并未去淮阴而被留在京城。
　　　Huaiyin: the native place of Han Xin, who however,
　　　was kept as a hostage in the capital after he was
　　　enfeoffed. Huaiyin was located in the north of
　　　present-day Jiangsu Province.

羽翼已成

yǔyì yǐ chéng

The Wings Are Fully Grown

　　刘邦当皇帝之后,宠爱戚(Qī)夫人,想废太子刘盈立戚夫人所生的刘如意为太子。后来刘盈用张良的计谋,请来了四位当时著名的隐士辅佐他,并且有意使刘邦见到他们跟随自己。刘邦感到十分惊讶,问他们:"我请你们来请了几年,但是你们都避开我,现在为什么跟随我的儿子呢?"这四位隐士说:"陛下轻视士人①,喜欢骂人,我们不愿受你的羞辱,所以逃避。我们听说太子为人仁孝,对士人恭敬重视,所以我们就来了。"刘邦说:"那就请你们尽心帮助太子吧。"刘邦对戚夫人说:"我本想换太子,但是太子有这四个人辅佐,羽翼已成,不能更动了。"因此太子终于未被更换。

　　后世用"羽翼已成"来比喻已经得到辅佐之人,势力已壮大,地位稳固。

After Liu Bang became Emperor, he favored a concubine named Lady Qi (戚) and wanted to depose Crown Prince Liu Ying (刘盈) from his position as heir to the throne in favor of Lady Qi's son Liu Ruyi (刘如意).

Liu Ying was advised by Zhang Liang to invite four famous hermits to join his entourage. Liu Bang was amazed at this, and said to the four, "I have been inviting you to attend me for many years, but you persistently refused to do so. Now I see you attending my son." These four answered, "Your Majesty despises thinkers, and is fond of abusing them. So we avoided you in order to avert insults. We have heard that the Crown Prince is kind and is a dutiful son. He respects and attaches importance to thinkers, so we have attached ourselves to him. " Liu Bang could only say, "Then please attend the Crown Prince well. " Then Liu Bang told Lady Qi, "I did want to replace the Crown Prince, but as he has these four wise hermits to escort him, his wings are now fully grown and so he can not be replaced. "

Later, this metaphor came to be used to indicate that somebody has obtained help and become strong, making his position secure.

注：① 士人：古代称读书人。
　　　Scholar.

萧规曹随

Xiāo guī Cáo suí

Cao Can Follows Xiao He's Rules

公元前 193 年,汉朝丞相萧何去世,死前推荐曹参为丞相。曹参上任后,一切都按萧何所定法规施行,不加更动,平日只是饮酒作乐。有一次上朝时皇帝刘盈问他为什么这样。曹参反问刘盈:"陛下自以为智慧和能力和高皇帝①相比怎样呢?"刘盈说:"我怎能和高皇帝相比呢!"曹参又问:"陛下以为我的才能和萧何比怎样?"刘盈说:"你似乎不如他。"曹参说:"陛下说得对,高皇帝和萧何平定天下,法令都订好了,只要我们尽职,遵照以前的规定办就是了。"刘盈说:"说得对,就照你说的办。"

后世以"萧规曹随"来比喻接手人遵守前人所定规矩施行。

In 193 B.C. Han Dynasty Prime Minister Xiao He passed away. On his deathbed he recommended Cao Can (曹参) as his successor. Upon taking office, Cao Can followed all Xiao He's regulations to the letter, and made not the slightest innovation. This naturally left him much spare time, which he passed in merrymaking. Displeased with his new prime minister's easy-going ways, the emperor, Liu Ying (刘盈), took him to task one day.

In his own defense, Cao Can asked his master, "How would Your Highness compare your wisdom and ability to that of the Great Emperor (Liu Bang, Liu Ying's father and founder of the Han Dynasty)?"

The emperor replied, nonplussed, "How could I compare myself to the Great Emperor?"

Thereupon, Cao Can asked, "How would Your Highness compare my abilities with those of my predecessor Xiao He?"

Liu Ying replied, "It seems to me that you are far inferior to the late prime minister."

Cao Can thereupon said, "Your Majesty speaks truly. The Great Emperor and Xiao He between them pacified the empire. Moreover, they enacted all the laws and regulations for ruling it. Our duty is to respect to the utmost their stipulations. If only we do so, all will be well."

The emperor was convinced. "It shall be as you say," he conceded.

Later, the expression, "Cao Can follows Xiao He's rules" came to apply to a successor who follows to the hilt the guidelines laid down by his predecessor.

注:① 高皇帝:指刘邦。

The Great Emperor: Liu Bang.

左袒　　偏袒

zuǒ tǎn　　piāntǎn

Loosening the Left Sleeve

公元前 195 年汉朝皇帝刘邦死后，皇后吕雉
(zhì) 专权，她逐步将政权和军权转到吕氏族人手
中，企图建立吕氏王朝。吕雉在公元前 180 年死去
时，她的侄子吕禄等人掌握着兵权。

太尉周勃①策划消灭诸吕，传令军中说："支持
刘家的褪下左袖 (左袒)，支持吕家的褪下右袖 (右
袒)。"结果全军都褪下了左袖，表示拥护刘氏王
朝。周勃随即派兵将吕氏全部杀掉。不久，刘邦与
一个妃子生的儿子刘恒被立为皇帝。

后世因此以"偏袒"来表示偏向某一方。

Following the death of the first Han Dynasty emperor,
Liu Bang, in 195 B. C. the reins of power fell into the hands
of his empress, Lü Zhi (吕雉). This woman lost no time
putting members of her family into dominant governmental
positions, with the intention of setting up a new dynasty of
the Lü clan.

When Lü Zhi died in 180 B. C. her nephews, led by Lü
Lu (吕禄), seized control of the military. At this juncture a
brother and a grandson of Liu Bang raised a revolt against the
Lü clan in order to restore the Lius to power.

Meanwhile, Zhou Bo, the commander-in-chief of the
Han armies, was smarting under the arrogant rule of the Lüs,
and was looking for a way to oust them. So one day he as-
sembled all his forces and ordered them, "All who support
the Liu family, loosen your left sleeves!" This was immedi-

ately followed by "All who support the Lü clan, loosen your right sleeves!" Thereupon, the whole army — to a man — displayed a sea of loosened left sleeves.

The upshot was that the usurpers were massacred, and Liu Heng, a son of Liu Bang, was put on the throne.

Later, "loosening the left sleeve" came to mean taking sides or being partial.

注：① 太尉周勃：统领全国军队的最高官员，但当时周勃无实权。

Although Zhou Bo had the title as the supreme commander of the national armed forces, he actually had no real power.

金屋藏娇

jīn wū cáng jiāo

Keeping a Beauty in a Golden House

此典出自班固①《汉武故事》。汉武帝刘彻(公元前 156—前 87) 四岁时，长公主把他抱到膝上，问他想不想要媳妇，他说他想要。长公主就指着她的女儿阿娇问："阿娇好吗？"刘彻笑着说："好。如果能得到阿娇做媳妇，我要盖一座金屋子让她住。"刘彻当了皇帝以后果然立阿娇为皇后。但是后来汉武帝另宠一妃，就把这个皇后废了。

后世用"金屋藏娇"这句话来说纳妾或养女人。

This anecdote is taken from *Stories of Emperor Wu of the Han Dynasty*, by Ban Gu.

When Liu Che (刘彻) (156 – 87 B.C.), who later became Emperor Wu, was four years old, the senior princess sat him on her knee and asked him if he wanted a wife. He answered yes. Then the princess pointed to her daughter Ajiao, and asked, "How about Ajiao?" Liu Che chuckled, and said, "She is lovely! If I can have Ajiao for my wife, I shall ensconce her in a golden house." When Liu Che succeeded to the throne, he made Ajiao his empress. But later he put her aside and bestowed his favors on a concubine.

Later, this expression came to be used to refer to taking a concubine or keeping a mistress.

注:① 班固:(公元 32—92),汉代史学家。
Ban Gu (32-92): a historian of Han Dynasty.

门可罗雀

mén kě luó què

You Can Catch Sparrows on the Doorstep

罗:张网捕(鸟)。 To catch (birds) with a net.

汉朝翟（Zhái）方进做最高法官——廷尉时，他家的宾客盈门。当他一度被罢了官的时候，宾客都不来了，门外冷静得可以设罗网捕雀（"门可罗雀"）。后来他又恢复官职，宾客们想再来。他在门上用大字写道："一死一生，乃①知交情；一贫一富，乃知交态②；一贵一贱，交情乃见③（xiàn）。"

后世以"门可罗雀"表示无人来往。

When Zhai Fangjin （翟方进）was minister of justice during the Han Dynasty, his house was always crowded with sycophants. But later, he was removed from his post for a time, and visitors became so few and far between that it was said that one could catch sparrows on his doorstep.

When he resumed his post, people once more flocked to him to ask for favors. Zhai stuck a notice on his gatepost, which said in big characters: "Friendship is tested at a critical moment of life and death; the ways of the world can be known in the alternation of poverty and riches; changes between illustriousness and lowliness reveal the true human relationships."

Later, the allusion "You can catch sparrows on the doorstep" came to be used to indicate that a person is isolated or shunned.

注：① 乃：副词"才"的意思。
An adverb, meaning "just".

② 交态:朋友间相处的情状、态度。
Relations and feelings between friends.

③ 见:表露在外面。
Shown on the outside.

牛郎织女

niúláng zhīnǚ

The Cowherd and the Weaving Girl

鹊桥

què qiáo

Building a Bridge of Magpies

此典来自民间故事。传说天上有七个为天庭纺织的仙女。有一天,她们来到尘世上的一处泉水里洗浴。一个放牛郎发现了她们,偷去了最小仙女的天衣。这位仙女不能再回天上,就和放牛郎结成了夫妻。后来玉帝①发现此事,就派天兵把织女捉回天上。牛郎跟着追到天上,王母娘娘看见他快要追上了,就拔出簪(zān)子②在他们之间划了一道线,这道线变成了天河,把牛郎和织女隔在河两边。王母娘娘只准他们每年七月七日半夜过河相会。喜鹊同情他们,聚集起来在天河上搭成一道桥,使牛郎和织女可以踏着鹊桥过河相会。

现在用牛郎织女比喻分居两地的夫妻或情人。用搭鹊桥比喻做媒或促使夫妻会合。

These phrases have their origin in a folk tale.

The story goes that seven fairy weavers who served the court of the Jade Emperor one day descended to Earth to bathe in a terrestrial spring. A young cowherd who was passing by happened to spy them, and stole the clothes of the youngest. As a consequence, she could not return to Heaven, but stayed on Earth as the cowherd's wife.

When the Jade Emperor learned of this he sent his guards down to Earth to drag the weaving girl back to Heaven. The cowherd followed her, but was spotted before he could catch up with his wife by the Queen Mother of Heaven. The latter drew a silver hairpin from her tresses and drew a line in the sky to separate the pair. This line then became the Milky Way (known in Chinese as the Silver River or Celestial River). The Queen Mother of Heaven permitted the Cowherd and the Weaving Maid to see each other only once a year — on the seventh day of the seventh month at midnight. But the two lovers were still separated by the Silver River. Their plight stirred the compassion of all the magpies on Earth, who flew up into the sky on that night and formed a bridge with their wings over the Silver River so that the Cowherd and the Weaving Maid could meet.

Later, the expression "the Cowherd and the Weaving Girl" came to be used to refer to husband and wife or lovers who have to live apart, and "building a bridge of magpies" means arranging a love match.

注:① 玉帝:玉皇大帝,道教称天上最高的神。
The short form for Yuhuang Dadi, the Supreme Deity of Taoism.

② 簪子:别住发髻(jì)的条状物,用金属、骨头、玉石等制成。
Hairpin made of metal, bones or jade, etc.

鹏程万里

péng chéng wàn lǐ

The Roc Flies Ten Thousand *Li*

《庄子》里有一个寓言,说北海有一种鱼叫做鲲 (kūn),它大得不可测量,这种鱼又变成鸟叫做鹏,鹏也大得不可测量。鹏要迁到南海时,扑击三千里的水面,乘着旋风盘旋上升九万里。鹏背 (bēi)负着青天,然后向南飞,翅膀像天上的云。

现在将"鹏程万里"用于祝愿人前途远大、事业壮伟。

The classic of Daoist philosophy named after its author Zhuang Zi (369-286 B. C.) contains the following anecdote:

There was once an enormous fish called the Kun(鲲) living in the North Sea. It changed into a huge bird called the Peng (鹏), or roc. The roc decided to fly the immeasurable distance to the South Sea. As it soared up to 90 thousand *li* in the sky, everything on the Earth appeared tiny. But, supported by the wind, it eventually reached its destination after a six-month journey.

Later, the expression, "The roc flies ten thousand *li*" came to be used to wish a person a promising future and great success.

注: 由第五十二个故事到第六十二个故事取材自《庄子》。《庄子》是集庄子(约公元前369—前286)和他的门人写的哲学文章而成的书,是道家经典之一。文章多采用寓言故事形式,想象丰富。

The anecdotes from here to the 62nd are adapted from

Zhuang Zi, one of the classics of Daoism. Most essays in the book are imaginative parables.

鼓盆之戚

gǔ pén zhī qī

The Sorrow of Drumming on the Basin

戚:悲哀,忧愁。 Sorrow, sadness.

庄子的妻子死了,他的朋友惠子去悼念,看见庄子坐在地上敲着盆子(鼓盆)唱歌,惠子就说:"妻子与你共同生活,养育子女,她也渐渐年老。现在她死去,你不哭也就可以了,还要敲着盆子唱歌,不是太过分了吗?"庄子说:"不是这样,她刚死时我难道不悲痛么,但是想到她原来不存在,以后才有了形体、生命,现在又死去,就像四季交替一样。如今她安静地躺在大屋子里,而我在旁边嗷嗷地哭,我想这样是不懂自然的规律,所以就不哭了。"

后世以"鼓盆之戚"来表示丧妻之悲。

When Zhuang Zi's wife died, his friend Hui Zi (惠子) went to offer his condolences to the sage. He saw Zhuang Zi sitting on the ground, drumming on an upturned basin and singing. Hui Zi said to him, "Your wife lived with you, and gave birth to and brought up your children. The fact that you refuse to weep just because she became old and died is something that I can understand. But to drum on a basin and sing — is that not going beyond the bounds of decorum?" Zhuang Zi answered, "That is not the case. When she died, of course I was grieved. But I realized that originally she did not exist. Then she had a shape and life, and then she died. That was just like the changing of the four seasons. Now she is quietly lying in a big room. If I weep and wail, that shows that I do not understand the rules of nature. So I ceased weeping. "

Later, "the sorrow of drumming on the basin" came to be used to describe sorrow over the death of one's wife.

相濡以沫

xiāng rú yǐ mò

Moistening Each Other With Saliva

濡：沾湿。　To moisten.

沫：唾沫。　Saliva, spittle.

庄子在一篇文章中说，泉水干了，鱼群被困在干地上，于是互相吹湿气、吐沫来保持湿润。

后世以"相濡以沫"来比喻人们在困境中以微小的力量互相帮助、照顾。

Zhuang Zi wrote in an essay: a certain spring dried up, and the fishes were stranded together on the dry bed of the spring. They moistened each other with their own saliva.

Later, the phrase "moistening each other with saliva" came to be used to describe people in distress helping and comforting each other with what little they have.

每下愈况，每况愈下

měi xià yù kuàng, měi kuàng yù xià

The Lower, the More Accurate the Comparison Is

况：比较对照。 To compare.

有人问庄子:"所谓的'道'在什么地方?"

庄子说:"无所不在。"那人又问:"请说得明确一些。"

"在蝼蛄(lóugū)蚂蚁之中。"

"怎么这样卑下呢?"

"在稊稗(tíbài)①之中。"

"怎么更卑下了呢?"

"在砖头瓦片之中。"

"怎么又进一步了呢?"

"在屎尿之中。"问的人不再说话了。

庄子说:"你的问题没有接触'道'的实质。管理市场的人用脚踩猪以测肥瘦,越向猪的下面——即脚胫处踩,就越测得准(每下愈况)。"

庄子的意思是越从低微的事物上探求,越能看出真实情况。后世用作"每况愈下",形容处境或情况越来越坏。

Someone once asked Zhuang Zi, "Where is the *Dao* (道) you are always talking about?"

Zhuang Zi answered, "It is omnipresent."

The man persisted, "Please be more explicit."

"It is in the crickets and the ants."

"Why so low?"

"It is in the weeds and the grass."

"Why even lower?"

"It is in the tiles and the bricks. "

"Why do you seek lower and lower comparisons?"

"It is in dung and urine. "

The men lapsed into silence.

Zhuang Zi said, "Your questions do not touch the essence of the *Dao*. When the market supervisor checks how fat a pig is by stepping on it, the lower part of the body he touches, the more accurate the check is. "

What Zhuang Zi meant was that the more humble the investigated objects are, the more truth can be obtained.

Later, the phrase "The lower, the more accurate the comparison is" came to be used to describe situations or conditions which are steadily deteriorating.

注:① 稊稗:稗子和稊都是田间杂草。

　　Weeds.

枯鱼之肆

kū yú zhī sì

Dried Fish Market

肆:铺子。 Shop, store.

庄子家里很穷,到一个官员处借粮食,那个官员说:"好,等我得到封地的税金以后就给你三百镒(yì)①金子,好吗?"庄子面带怒色说:"我来的时候,有一条鲫鱼在干车辙中叫我,说它是东海水臣,问我能不能用一点儿水救活它。我说:'我去要求吴越②的国王,发西江的水来接你,好吗?'鲫鱼生气地说:'我离开了我的家乡,没有容身的地方。现在有一点儿水就可以活下去,而你却这样说,那还不如早点到干鱼市场去找我'。"

后世以此话来比喻对处境困难的人,只是口头上许给好处,实际上做不到。

Zhuang Zi, being impoverished, once approached a wealthy government official for a loan. The official said, "As soon as the taxes are all gathered in from my estates I will lend you 300 *yi* of gold. Will that be enough for you?"

Perceiving that this was an excuse to fob him off, Zhuang Zi retorted angrily, "On my way here I saw a carp lying in a dry ditch. The carp called out to me, saying that he was an official of the emperor of the East Sea. He asked me to bring him a bucket of water to save his life. I replied that I would hasten to ask the kings of Wu and Yue to release the waters of the West River, which would flow down to where he was lying gasping, and thus save his life. The carp said angrily, 'I left my home and now have no place to stay. Only a little water can save my life. If you say so, you'd better go and look for me in the dried fish market.'"

Later, the phrase "dried fish market" came to mean a situation in which a person in dire straits receives only promises of help and not concrete assistance.

注:① 镒:古代重量单位,约合二十两。

An ancient unit of weight, equivalent to about 20 *liang*.

② 吴越:吴国和越国,古代建在南方的小国。

Two small ancient states in southeast China.

庖丁解牛

páodīng jiě niú

Butchering an Ox

游刃有余

yóu rèn yǒu yú

Having Plenty of Room for the Play of the Butcher's Cleaver

庖丁:厨师。 Cook.

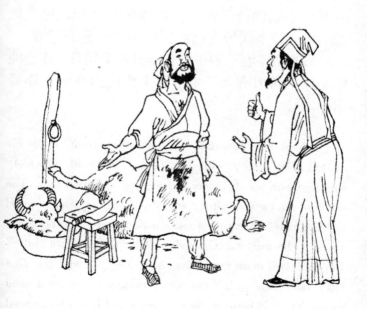

　　厨师为他的主人分解牛体,他用手推脚踩,肩膀靠、膝盖顶。用刀割时发出声音,牛体分裂也发出声音,这些声音有如音乐,他的动作有如舞蹈。主人说:"啊,技术竟然如此精良!"厨师放下刀说:"我喜爱'道'胜于技术。我现在用精神工作,依照牛体的结构去分开筋肉、骨头相连的地方。刀刃好像没有厚度,而这些相连处都有间隙(xì),以没有厚度的东西进入有间隙的地方,刀刃自然可以活动有余(游刃有余),所以我的刀用了十九年还好像才磨的一样。虽然这样,遇到难分开的地方,我还要小心地慢慢动作,使牛体顺利分开,摊在地上。我这时才能为自己已完成的工作感到满意。"

　　后世以"庖丁解牛"来形容技术精良、技艺纯熟。用"游刃有余"来形容工作能力高于工作要求。

A cook was dismembering the carcass of an ox for his master. He pushed with his hands, trod with his feet, squeezed with his shoulders and pressed with his knees. The sound of the cleaver cutting and of the carcass being severed was like music, and the cook's actions were like those of a dancer. His master exclaimed, "Oh, what elegant skill!" The cook laid down his cleaver and said, "I love the *Dao* (道) more than skill. I am now working with my mind, and let the intervals between flesh, sinews and bones be severed according to their natural structure. The edge of the cleaver seems to have no thickness, but space exists between all the animal's joints. When something with no thickness enters a place with space, there will always be enough room for it to move freely. So though my cleaver has been used for nineteen years, it is as keen as if it had just been sharpened. But at places hard to cut, I have to move with care, to make sure that the carcass is cut up smoothly and spread on the ground. Only then can I enjoy the satisfaction of accomplishing the job. "

Later, the expression "butchering an ox" came to be used to describe an elegant and well-practiced skill. "Having plenty of room for the play of the butcher's cleaver" is used to describe a person who is more than equal to a task or who does a job with practiced skill and ease.

徒劳无功
tú láo wú gōng

劳而无功
láo ér wú gōng

Working Hard But to No Avail

徒劳：白费力气。 Wasting one's efforts.

这个典故来自庄子的一段议论。

庄子认为古今情况不同，不可以在当代推行古代的制度。各时代应有不同的办法。三皇五帝①的办法各不相同，但是却同样能治理国家。有如各种水果不同，但是都可口。而如果给猴子穿上周公②的衣服，猴子必定把衣服抓碎扯光，因为猴子与周公不同。又如在陆地上行舟、水里走车，不但徒劳无功还要自己受害。

后世用"徒劳无功"或"劳而无功"表示费力去做没有成效的事或出了力却没有成效。

This allusion comes from a comment by Zhuang Zi, when he wished to emphasize that there were differences between the past and the present; ancient institutions could not be used in later times. Different times should employ different ways. He said the methods used by "the Three Supremes and the Five Emperors" were different, but all of them achieved success in governing the country. Just as fruits may be different, yet they are all palatable. If a monkey were to be dressed in the clothes of the Marquis of Zhou (周公), it would certainly tear them into pieces, for the monkey would be different from the Marquis of Zhou. So to use ancient institutions in later times was like sailing a boat on land or driving a cart in water – one would not only work to no avail, but also harm oneself.

Later, the phrase "working hard but to no avail" came

to be used to denote doing a hard but fruitless job, or working hard with no gain.

注:① 三皇五帝:传说中的远古君主。

The Three Supremes and Five Emperors: legendary monarchs in remote antiquity. They were regarded as ideal rulers.

② 周公:姓姬名旦, 周朝初年的政治家, 周武王的弟弟。中国封建时代认为周公是圣人。

The Marquis of Zhou: named Ji Dan, a leading figure during the early Zhou Dynasty, and a younger brother of Emperor Wu of Zhou (周武王). The Marquis of Zhou was regarded a sage throughout Chinese history.

视为畏途

shì wéi wèi tú

Regarded as a Dangerous Road

视:看待。   To regard.

庄子有一段议论养生之道的话。意思是说对精神和身体的保养都要顾及，偏废哪一面都不行。比如有一条凶险的路(畏途)，一家人有十分之一的人在那里被杀了，父子兄弟就会互相警告，出门时一定要带着武器结伴而行。但是现在很多人只注意这些明显的较小的危险，而忽视了更大的危险。比如多少人死于卧席上、饮食之间无休止的享乐，真是太可怕了。

后世以"视为畏途"表示把事情或过程看做是危险可怕的。

Zhuang Zi once talked about the way to keep in good health. His central idea was that the soundness of both mind and body should be cared for. Neither can be ignored.

For example, when a road is infested with fierce bandits where one-tenth of a family have been killed, father and son, and elder and younger brothers warn each other about the danger. If any of them wants to go out, they travel together in an armed group. However, many people emphasize only these obvious and smaller dangers, but ignore larger ones, such as dying early because of excessive pleasure-seeking, eating and drinking. Zhuang Zi said that such excesses should be regarded as just as dangerous as a bandit-ridden road.

Later, the phrase is used to mean that the process of doing something is regarded as potentially dangerous and risk-taking.

越俎代庖

yuè zǔ dài páo

Abandoning the Sacrificial Vessels for the Saucepans

越：超出某个范围。To go beyond a certain scope.

俎：古代祭祀时盛祭肉的器具。 An ancient vessel used to hold sacrificial offerings.

这典故来自庄子写的一个寓言。

寓言说帝尧 (Yáo) 时有一个隐士许由，帝尧听说许由非常有贤德，于是去要求许由接受帝位。许由听了以后对帝尧说："你在帝位已经把天下治理好了，我为什么要代替你呢? 厨师即使不做饭，祭师也不应当抛开祭器去代替他工作 ("越俎代庖")。"

后世以"越俎代庖"来描述越权行事或做了应由别人做的工作。

This allusion comes from a fable attributed to Zhuang Zi.

The fable goes that in the time of Emperor Yao (尧帝), there was a hermit named Xu You (许由). The emperor heard that he was very virtuous, so he offered him the throne. Xu You said to the emperor, "You had governed well, so why should I replace you? Even when the cook does not cook, the priest should not abandon the sacrificial vessels to meddle instead with the saucepans."

Later, the phrase "abandoning the sacrificial vessels for the saucepans" came to be used to mean exceeding one's function and interfering in another's affairs, or usurping somebody else's function.

注：帝尧：传说中远古时的帝王。传说那时帝位的继承是用禅 (shàn) 让的办法。

Emperor Yao: a legendary emperor of remote antiquity. There was a tradition of sagerulers abdicating in favor of those they cousidered wiser than themselves at that time.

得心应手

dé xīn yìng shǒu

The Hands Respond to the Heart

此典出自《庄子·天道》。

一个国王在院子里看书，一个做轮子的工人说国王看的只是古人的糟粕(zāopò)①。国王发怒了，让轮工讲出道理，否则就处死他。轮工说："我是从我做的工作悟出这个道理的。做轮子时用力要恰到好处，否则轮子就不合适。至于怎样用力才最恰当只能心里知道，再用在手上("得心应手")，这种感觉是无法告诉别人的。所以我的感觉不能传给儿子，儿子也不能从我这里得到这种感觉。古人和他们不能用语言传达的感觉都死去了，所以你读的书只是古人留下的糟粕。"

后人用"得心应手"来描述经验丰富、技术精湛(zhàn)和工作熟练。

This allusion is exerpted from Zhuang Zi's *Heavenly Doctrine*:

Duke Huan of Qi was reading in the garden, when a wheelwright who was working there asked him what he was reading. When the duke told him, the wheelwright said, "What you are reading is nothing more than the lees and scum of bygone men." Angered, the duke demanded that he explain, otherwise, he would be executed. The wheelwright said, "I get the truth from my work. The strength used in making wheels has to be just right, or the wheels will not fit properly. But what is the precise strength? I feel it in my heart, and my hands respond to it. It cannot be expressed in words. So I cannot pass this kind of intuition on to my son, and my son cannot get it from me. The ancients and their inexpressible feelings died together. So that is why I say that what you are reading is only the dregs left by them."

Later, the phrase "The hands respond to the heart" came to be used to describe rich experience, consumate skill and working with facility.

注:① 糟粕:酒糟、豆渣之类的东西。比喻粗劣而没有价值的东西。
Waste matter; dregs.

泼水难收

pō shuǐ nán shōu

Spilt Water Cannot Be Retrieved

此典出自民间故事及《汉书·朱买臣传》。

朱买臣年轻时家里很穷，他的妻子弃他而去。后来朱买臣逐渐升了高官，并被任命为他故乡的太守。有一次他在路上遇到前妻和她的后夫，就将他们带回官署。后来朱买臣的前妻要求复婚。朱买臣把水泼在地上向她说，如果你能把泼了的水收回来，就可以复婚。

后世用"泼水难收"来比喻已成定局的事，不可挽回。

This allusion originates partly in folklore and partly from "the Biography of Zhu Maichen (朱买臣)" in the *History of the Han Dynasty*.

Zhu Maichen was very poor when he was young. Seeing no future for him, his wife left him. His fortunes revived, however, and he was appointed governor of his home region. Once, he met his former wife and her second husband in the street. The woman asked him to take her back, but Zhu Maichen splashed water on the ground, and told her if she could retrieve the water, their marriage could be resumed. Soon after that, the woman committed suicide.

Later, this allusion came to be used to describe an irrevocable action or decision.

死灰复燃

sǐ huī fù rán

Dying Embers May Glow Again

汉朝时有一个官员叫韩安国,有过功劳,但因为犯法被关在牢中。狱官田甲故意侮辱他。韩安国对他说:"难道死灰就不会再烧起来吗("死灰独不复燃乎")?"田甲说:"如果烧起来就用尿浇灭。"后来韩安国恢复了职位,田甲吓得逃跑了。韩安国传令说:"如果田甲不回来就杀他全家。"田甲只好回来请求宽恕,韩安国对他说:"你值得我报复吗?"以后他对田甲很好。

后世用"死灰复燃"形容被消灭的势力重新出现或失势的人重新得势。

In the Han Dynasty there was an official named Han Anguo (韩安国). Despite great achievements he was imprisoned for an offense. The prison warder Tian Jia (田甲) treated his new charge harshly. Han Anguo warned him, saying, "Is it not pssible for dying embers to glow again?" Tian Jia retorted, "If they do, I will urinate on them and put then out again." Soon afterwards, Han Anguo was released and re-instated in his high office.

Thereupon, Tian Jia fled in dread. Han Anguo threatened to execute the prison warder's whole family if he did not return. So Tian Jia surrendered and begged for pardon. Han Anguo laughed and said to him "Are you worth my reprisal?" and treated him well afterwards.

Later, "Dying embers may glow again" came to be used to describe a person or cause which seems to be defeated but which may spring back to become a potent force once more.

投笔从戎

tóu bǐ cóngróng

Exchanging the Writing Brush for the Sword

从:从事,参加。To engage in, join.

戎:军事,军队。Military, army.

此典出自《后汉书·班超传》。

汉朝班超 (公元 32—102) 出身史官家庭。年轻时丧父，因为家贫就为官府抄写文书来奉养母亲。他曾将笔抛下，自叹说："大丈夫没有别的志愿，只想学傅介子①和张骞 (Qiān) ②在远方立功以取得爵位，怎能长久生活在笔砚之间！"以后他奉命出使西域③，使西域五十多个小国归附汉朝。他也被任命为西域都护，封定远侯。

后世用"投笔从戎"形容丢开文职去参加军队。

This story comes from the *History of the Later Han Dynasty*.

Ban Chao (班超 32-102 A. D.) was from a family of historians. His father died when he was young, and his family was so poor that he worked as a copy clerk for the government to provide for his mother. Once he threw down his writing brush, and sighed, "A true man should have no aspiration but to follow Fu Jiezi and Zhang Qian to win honor in foreign lands and gain a noble title. How can I molder away among writing brushes and inkstones?" Later, he was sent to the Western Region as an envoy, where he managed to get more than 50 kingdoms to pay allegiance to the Han emperor. He was appointed governor of the Western Region, and was given the title Marquis Ding Yuan.

Later, this phrase came to be used to describe the act of

giving up a civilian post and joining the army.

注:① 傅介子:汉代官员,曾出使西域大宛(wǎn)国,用
计斩西域鄯(Shàn)善国王,回朝后封义阳侯。

Fu Jiezi: an official of the Han Empire sent as an
envoy to Dawan (大宛 one of the kingdoms of the
Western Region), he schemed to assassinate the king
of Loulan (楼兰 another kingdom of the Western
Region), and was given the title of Marquis of Yiyang
(义阳).

② 张骞:汉代通西域使者。曾出使西域,使西域诸国
与汉朝通好,对交流两地文化多有建树,封为博望
侯。

Zhang Qian: an envoy of the Han Empire, sent to the
Western Region. He started the communications and
friendship between the Han Empire and the Western
Kingdoms, and was given the title of "Marquis of
Bowang" (博望).

③ 西域:古代指玉门关 (今甘肃省玉门市) 以西地
区。

The Western Region: the ancient name for the land
west of Yumenguan, at the present city of Yumen (玉
门) in Gansu Province.

不入虎穴，焉得虎子

bù rù hǔxué, yān dé hǔzǐ

You Must Enter the Tiger's Den to Catch His Cubs

班超带了三十六人奉命出使西域，到达鄯(Shàn)善国①。鄯善国王对他们很尊重，以上宾招待。后来匈奴②使者带着大批随员也到了鄯善。由于匈奴使者的挑拨，国王对班超等人变冷淡了，而且显出敌意。班超发现了这种变化的原因，就将众人召集起来说："我们现在的处境很危险。但是不进入虎穴，怎能捉到小老虎（'不入虎穴，焉得虎子'）？如果我们趁夜用火攻袭击匈奴使者，他们不知我们虚实，必然被消灭，我们也就安全了。"大家都同意这么办，于是班超率领他们趁夜突然袭击了匈奴使者的帐篷，匈奴使者和他的一百多个随从都被杀死。鄯善国王很害怕，班超向他说明利害，并好言相劝，于是鄯善国王诚心归顺了汉朝。

后世以"不入虎穴，焉得虎子"比喻不冒风险就不会有大收获。

When Ban Chao was an envoy to the Western Region, he once went to visit the king of Shanshan (鄯善) with a small entourage of only 36 men. The king treated him with the utmost hospitality, until an envoy from the Xiongnu arrived with a large retinue, whereupon he gave Ban Chao the cold-shoulder.

Realising that both his mission and he himself were in danger, Ban Chao devised a desperate plan: they would launch a surprise attack on the Xiongnu encampment at

night, beating gongs and setting fire to the tents. When the
Xiongnu rushed out in a panic, they would slay them. When
his men expressed alarm at such a perilous undertaking, Ban
Chao said, "How can you catch tiger cubs without first en-
tering the tiger's den?"

So they carried out the plan, annilhilated the
Xiongnu's tents and won the king of Shanshan's allegiance
to the Han emperor.

Later, the saying, "You must enter the tiger's den to
catch his cubs" came to be used to indicate that no great
enterprise can be successful without some risk being taken.

注:① 鄯善国:在今新疆维吾尔自治区鄯善县。
　　Shanshan: an ancient kingdom situated in
　　present-day Shanshan County in the Xinjiang Uygur
　　Autonomous Region.
② 匈奴:古代中国北方的一个强大的游牧民族。
　　Xiongnu: a powerful nomadic people in ancient
　　times, roaming the deserts of northwest China.

马革裹尸

mǎ gé guǒ shī

A Horsehide Shroud

此典出自《后汉书·马援传》。

马援(公元前 14—公元 49)是汉代名将。南北征战屡立战功。他曾说："大丈夫应当战死在疆(jiāng)场，用马皮裹着尸体下葬，怎能睡在床上在儿女照看中死去呢。"后来他在六十二岁时自请率军出征，在战场上他与士兵同守阵地，终于在第二年病死军中。

后人用"马革裹尸"来形容军人英勇战死疆场。

This allusion comes from the "Biography of Ma Yuan" in the *History of the Later Han Dynasty*.

Ma Yuan (马援 14 B. C. – 49 A. D.) was a leading general who, after spending decades campaigning, at the age of 62, persuaded the emperor to let him lead an army into battle once more, saying, "A real man should die in action and be buried in a horsehide shroud instead of being attended in bed by sons and daughters till his death." And sure enough, he died at his post the following year.

Later, the phrase, "a horsehide shroud" came to be used to mean dying heroically on the battlefield or sticking to one's post to the end.

小巫见大巫

xiǎo wū jiàn dà wū

A Junior Sorcerer in the Presence of a Great One

巫:旧时以祈神为职业的人。Sorcerer, witch.

此典出自《三国志》①。

汉朝末年有两个人叫张纮(Hóng)和陈琳。他们都是有才华的文学家，而且都很推崇对方的文采和作品，张纮给陈琳写信表示叹服他的文才。而陈琳回信说自己在张纮面前犹如"小巫见大巫"。这句话的原意是小巫师在大巫师面前不能施法，陈琳借此说自己的作品与张纮的作品相比就黯(àn)然失色。

后世用来比喻两者相比较，优劣、高下差得很远。

This story is excerpted from the *History of the Three Kingdoms*.

In the late Han Dynasty, there were two talented writers named Zhang Hong (张纮) and Chen Lin (陈琳). Both had great esteem for each other's literary talents and works. Zhang Hong once wrote a letter to Chen Lin expressing his admiration for his literary grace. The other wrote in reply saying that compared to Zhang Hong, he was like a junior sorcerer in the presence of a great one. The original meaning was that a junior sorcerer cannot make his magic effective before a great sorcerer. Chen Lin used this to denote that his literary works were eclipsed by those by Zhang Hong.

Later, this phrase came to be used to denote that when two things are compared, one is obviously superior to the other.

注：① 《三国志》：晋朝陈寿所著，记载三国时期的历史。

The *History of the Three Kingdoms*: written by Chen Shou in the Jin（晋） Dynasty, recording the history of the struggles between the kingdoms of Wei（魏）, Shu Han（蜀汉） and Wu（吴）.

举案齐眉

jǔ àn qí méi

Holding the Tray Up to the Eyebrows

案:古代进食用的木托盘。　A tray in ancient times.

梁鸿是东汉时的学者,他年轻时很穷,给人家放猪过活。他的妻子叫孟光,也是一位有学识的女人。

后来他们在吴地^①居住。梁鸿为人家舂(chōng)^②米谋生。每天回家后,他的妻子用托盘给他送饭时总是低着头把托盘举得和眉毛一样高,表示对丈夫的恭敬。古时把托盘叫"案",所以后世用"举案齐眉"形容夫妻相敬相爱。

Liang Hong (梁鸿) was a scholar of the Eastern Han (东汉) Dynasty. He was very poor when he was young, and earned his living as a swineherd. He married Meng Guang (孟光), a well educated woman. Later, they went to live in the State of Wu (吴). There Liang Hong husked rice for others to make a living. Every day when he came home, Meng Guang served him food with her head bowed and holding the tray up to her eyebrows to show repect for him.

Hence the phrase, "holding the tray up to the eyebrows" describes a couple having respect and love for each other.

注:① 吴地:江苏省南部和浙江省北部一带。
　　The area that covers the south of Jiangsu and the north of Zhejiang provinces.
　② 舂:把东西放在石臼里捣去皮壳或捣碎。
　　Pound, pestle.

捉刀

zhuō dāo

Holding the Sword

魏王曹操①将要接见匈奴使者。他认为自己长得不好看,不雄伟,不能让外人见了觉得威严可敬畏,就叫一位外貌雄伟的官员扮成魏王接见使者。他自己却持刀站在床头假装待卫。接见完毕后,他打发间谍去问匈奴使者觉得魏王怎么样。匈奴使者答道:"魏王仪态高雅,威望不凡,但在床头持刀的那个人,是个真正的英雄。"魏王听到这话就派人把那位使者杀了。

后世以"捉刀"表示代人作文。

Once Cao Cao, king of Wei, was about to receive an envoy from the Xiongnu tribe. Having doubts about his ability to inspire the envoy with sufficient awe, he made an imposing subordinate official pretend to be the king, while he himself stood beside the throne bearing a huge scimitar.

After the audience Cao Cao sent a spy to the envoy to ask "What do you think of the king of Wei?" The envoy answered, "The king of Wei had a polished and dignified bearing; but that man standing beside him holding a sword is a real hero." On hearing this, Cao Cao sent an assassin in pursuit of that envoy and had him killed.

Later, the phrase "holding the sword" means to write for and in the name of someone else.

注:① 曹操 (公元 155—220) 是东汉末年政治家、军事家。在国内战争中逐渐取得权力,并统一中国北

方。后来担任丞相,并被封为魏王。

Cao Cao (155-220 A. D.): a statesman and strategist of the late Eastern Han Dynasty. He gained power gradually in a series of civil wars and unified the northern parts of China. He later became the prime minister, and then was enfeoffed the King of Wei (魏).

万事俱备, 只欠东风

wàn shì jù bèi, zhǐ qiàn dōngfēng

All That Is Needed Is an East Wind

俱:全,都。 All.

此典出自《三国演义》①。

公元 208 年冬天，曹操带领大军南侵。孙权、刘备的联军在长江南岸列阵抵抗。他们策划火烧曹军的战船，当火攻的准备工作都做好了以后，他们才想起冬天的风都是由西北吹来的，如果用火攻，火就会烧自己的船，所以要用火攻曹军的战船就必须有东风（"万事俱备，只欠东风"）。这时刘备的军师诸葛亮说他可以呼唤东风，最后东风果然被他唤来了，曹操的军队被烧得大败。

后来，"万事俱备，只欠东风"用来比喻为完成一件事已做好准备，只缺某一个关键条件。

This allusion is taken from *The Romance of the Three Kingdoms*.

In the winter of 208 Cao Cao（曹操）led a large army on a southern campaign. The allied armies of Sun Quan（孙权）and Liu Bei（刘备）were massed on the south bank of the Yangtze River. They planned to attack the warships of Cao Cao with blazing barges. When all the preparations for the attack were completed, they called to mind that the wind in winter always blew from the northwest, and so would blow the fire barges back toward their own ships. So an east wind was needed for the attack. Zhuge Liang（诸葛亮）, the chief advisor of Liu Bei, said that he could summon an east wind, and he did so by trickery. The result was that Cao Cao's ships were burnt to ashes.

Later, "Everything is ready, and all that is needed is an east wind" came to be used to describe a situation in which all is ready except what is crucial for the fulfilment of an undertaking.

注:① 《三国演义》:元末明初罗贯中所著长篇小说。内容描写公元 220—280 年间,曹操、刘备、孙权及其继承人所统治的魏、蜀、吴三国之间的斗争。

The Romance of the Three Kingdoms: a novel written by Luo Guanzhong (1330-1400), which describes the conflicts between the three kingdoms of Wei, Shu and Wu ruled by Cao Cao, Liu Bei, Sun Quan and their successors, respectively, from 220 to 280.

鹤立鸡群

hè lì jī qún

Like a Crane Standing Among Chickens

　　晋朝的时候,有个人对王戎①说:"昨天在众人之中看见嵇绍,就是嵇康②的儿子。他神态昂扬,像野鹤立在鸡群中一样。"王戎说:"你是还没看见过他的父亲呐!"意思是嵇康比嵇绍更为出众。

　　后世以"鹤立鸡群"来比喻某人在人群中仪表或气质、才能突出。

Someone once told Wang Rong (王戎), "Yesterday I saw Ji Shao among a crowd of people. He looked so upright and lofty-spirited — like a wild crane standing proudly among chickens." Wang Rong replied, "You haven't yet seen his father!" He meant that Ji Shao's father, Ji Kang (嵇康), was even more outstanding than his son.

Later, the phrase "like a crane standing among chickens" came to be used to describe someone outstanding in appearance, disposition or talent among a crowd of inferiors.

注:①②嵇康、王戎:当时的名士。
　　Ji Kang and Wang Rong: famous scholars of that time.

乐不思蜀

lè bù sī Shǔ

So Happy That One Thinks No More of Shu

蜀：在四川省东部和云南、贵州省北部一带。An area in the eastern part of Sichuan Province, and northern parts of Yunnan and Guizhou provinces.

三国时代后期，公元 263 年蜀国灭亡，后主刘禅投降，被俘到魏都洛阳。

在魏国掌权的晋王司马昭（Zhāo）设宴招待刘禅，让人表演原来蜀国的歌舞给他看。旁人都感到很凄惨，而刘禅却照常嬉笑。

有一天，晋王问刘禅："想念蜀地吗？"刘禅回答说："这里很快乐，不想蜀地了（'此间乐不思蜀也'）。"

后世以"乐不思蜀"来形容某些人只顾一时享乐而忘却了自己的责任或故乡。

In the late period of the Three Kingdoms, the kingdom of Shu (蜀) was subjugated. Its ruler, Liu Chan (刘禅), surrendered and was taken to Luoyang (洛阳), the capital of the Kingdom of Wei.

Sima Zhao (司马昭), the ruler of Wei, gave a banquet in honor of Liu Chan, at which he deliberately arranged to have music and dancing from Shu as the entertainment. This saddened all the Shu captives, except for Liu Chan himself.

Later, Sima Zhao asked Liu Chan: "Do you not miss your homeland?" Liu Shan replied, "I am so happy here that I think no more of Shu."

Later, "so happy that one thinks no more of Shu" came to be used to speak of someone who indulges in pleasure to the extent that he forgets home and duty.

不为五斗米折腰

bù wèi wǔ dǒu mǐ zhéyāo

Won't Kowtow for Five *Dou* of Rice

斗：量粮食的器具，容量是十升。Dry measure for grain (one decaliter).

折腰：弯腰行礼。也指侍奉人。 To bow; also to wait on others.

晋朝的陶潜（公元 365—427）一名渊明，曾做彭泽①县县令。任职八十多天的时候，郡②里派督邮③来视察。县里的下属告诉陶渊明，他应该穿着官服束着袍带去见督邮。陶渊明叹息说："我不能为五斗米折腰向乡里小人。"当天就把官印交了回家去。

后世用"不为五斗米折腰"形容人有骨气，不肯为物质利益和地位屈从别人。

When the Jin (晋) Dynasty poet Tao Yuanming (陶渊明 365-427) was young he was appointed magistrate of Pengze (彭泽) County. He had not been in the postlong when a senior official came to inspect the county. Tao Yuanming's aide urged him to make haste and don his best regalia and go out to meet the visitor. Tao Yuanming there-upon retorted, "I will not dress myself up and kowtow to this pretentious bumpkin just for five *dou* of rice (referring to his salary as an official). " The very next day, he handed in his official seal and returned home.

Later, "won't kowtow for five *dou* of rice" came to be used to describe a person of ideals who will not humble himself for material gain.

注：① 彭泽县：在今江西省湖口县东。
　　Pengze County: in the east of the present Hukou (湖口) County in Jiangxi (江西) Province.

② 郡:统辖数县的行政单位。

An administrative unit in acient China, that governed several counties.

③ 督邮:郡守的佐吏,负责督察所统辖各县。

An assistant official of the prefectual magistrate, whose duty was to inspect the counties, in the prefecture.

桃花源

táohuā yuán

Land of Peach Blossoms

　　这个典故出自晋朝陶渊明写的一篇小说《桃花源记》，小说中说有一个渔人无意中来到武陵①桃花溪的源头，发现一处村落，这里人的祖先是在秦朝避兵乱而躲到这里的难民。他们已经在这里生活了好多代，与外界完全隔绝。他们不想与外界联系，也不想离开这里。渔人回家之后，报告了官府，也和别人说起那里的情况，但是他们再去找时就再也找不到那个地方了。

　　后世称偏僻、安乐的地方为桃花源。

This allusion comes from a story written by Tao Yuanming (陶渊明) of the Jin (晋) Dynasty (265-420).

The story goes that a fisherman came unexpectedly to the source of a stream, where he discovered a village inhabited by people whose ancestors had fled from the turbulence during the Qin (秦) Dynasty (221-206 B. C.). They were entirely isolated from the outside world, and had no wish for any contact with it. When the fisherman returned home he told the local magistrate and his neighbors about the place. But when they went to look for this idyllic village they could not find it.

Later, a remote and peaceful place came to be called a Land of Peach Blossoms.

注:①　武陵:今湖南省常德市西。

Wuling: at the west of the present-day Changde City in Hunan Province.

一人得道，鸡犬升天

yī rén dé dào,　jī quǎn shēngtiān

When a Man Attains the *Dao*, Even His Pets Go to Heaven

　　有个神话故事说，晋代人许逊跟仙人学得秘法和法术。他活到一百三十岁时，全家人一起升天，连家中鸡狗也一同飞升而去。

　　《神仙传》中还有个故事说，汉代淮南王刘安吃了炼成的丹药升天，鸡狗吃了剩下的药也升了天。

　　后世以"一人得道，鸡犬升天"来比喻某些人有了权势，和他有关系的人都能跟着沾光。

Xu Xun (许逊) of the Jin (晋) Dynasty was said to have learned magic arts from immortals and lived to the age of one hundred and thirty years. When he died, his whole family, including even their chickens and dogs, ascended to Heaven together with him.

Stories of the Immotals contains a similar anecdote: The King of Huainan (淮南) took a magic elixir and ascended to Heaven. The dogs and chickens that ate the remains of the elixir flew up to Heaven too.

Later, the allusion "When a man attains the *Dao*, even his pets go to Heaven" came to be used satirically to describe how when a person gains power, all his relatives and friends tend to benefit too.

沧海桑田

cānghǎi sāngtián

**Seas Change Into Mulberry Orchards, and
Mulberry Orchands Into Seas**

此典出自《神仙传》①。

《神仙传》中有一段神仙王远和女神仙麻姑的对话。麻姑对王远说："自从我们认识以来，已经看到东海三次变为桑田，这次我去蓬莱②，看到海水又变浅了，只有往日一半深，恐怕又要变成桑田了吧。"王远说："我也听见圣人说，海中又要扬起尘土了。"

后世以这个典故来形容世事、人事的翻覆变迁或形容年代久远。

This allusion is from *Stories of the Immortals* (神仙传). Female immortal Magu (麻姑) once said to male immortal Wang Yuan (王远), "Since we first got to know each other, I have thrice seen the East Sea change into mulberry orchards. When I went to Penglai last time, I saw the sea had become shallow again, the depth being only half of what it usually is. I am afraid it will soon become mulberry orchards again."

Wang Yuan answered, "I have heard from a sage that dust is going to replace the sea."

This phrase is used to refer to the upheavals and great changes in the world and in human lives, or the passing of time.

注:① 《神仙传》:为三、四世纪之间方士葛洪所著。

　　Stories of the Immortals: written by a necromancer
　　Ge Hong between the third and fourth centuries.

② 蓬莱:传说中东海里神仙所住的仙山。

　　Penglai: a legendary hill in the East Sea, where
　　immortals lived.

阿堵物

ā dǔ wù

Those Things

晋代有个王衍自命清高，平时绝不提"钱"字。他的妻子不同意他这种态度，有一天王衍睡着了，她就叫人在他的床周围堆满了钱，想着他睡醒走不出来，一定要叫人把钱搬走，这样他就不得不说"钱"字了。王衍醒来，却叫人把"阿堵物"搬走，还是没有说"钱"字。"阿堵物"的意思是那些东西，是当时的口语。

后世以"阿堵物"作为钱的别称。

Wang Yan（王衍）of the Jin（晋）Dynasty regarded himself as a man aloof from all worldly considerations. In particular, he would never mention the word "money." His wife was most annoyed about this. Once, when Wang Yan was asleep, she sent servants to pile coins around him, thinking that when he woke up he would have to call the servants to remove the coins, and thus have to say the word "money." But when Wang Yan awoke, he just said, "Take those things（阿堵物, a colloquialism of that time）away." He was determined not to utter the word "money" at all.

Later, "those things" came to be used as another name for money.

白面书生

bái miàn shūshēng

Pale-Faced Scholars

公元450年,南北朝时,南朝的宋朝将军沈庆之被任命统管全部军事部署。当时宋朝皇帝认为可以向北朝的魏朝进攻,而沈庆之认为自己的军队不如魏军,进攻必定失败。皇帝看到不能说服沈庆之,就让两个文臣和他辩论。沈庆之发怒说:"治国有如治家,种田的事要问佣人,纺织的事应当问婢(bì)女,现在陛下讨论要不要进攻北方,却要这些'白面书生'来谋划,事情怎能办好呢?"

后世用"白面书生"指年轻不了解世事的读书人。

In 450 A. D. Shen Qingzhi (沈庆之) was made commander-in-chief of the forces of the Song Dynasty of the Northern and Southen Dynasties (420-589). The Song emperor wanted to invade the territory of Wei (魏), to the north, but Shen Qingzhi argued that the army of Song was inferior to that of Wei. The Emperor told two civilian courtiers to debate the matter with him. Shen Qingzhi thereupon became angry, and said, "Ruling a state is like keeping a house. One should ask the hired men about farming, and ask the maids about weaving. Now Your Majesty wants to discuss an invasion of the north with these pale-faced scholars! That is preposterous".

Later, the phrase "pale-faced scholars" came to be used to refer to young scholars who know little about real life.

洛阳纸贵

Luòyáng zhǐ guì

Paper Is Expensive in Luoyang

这个典故出自《晋书》。

西晋文学家左思（约公元 250—305），精心构思，字斟（zhēn）句酌（zhuó），用了十年时间写成《三都赋（fù）①》。写成后，经过当时几位著名文学家的推荐，被首都洛阳的知识界和官员们争相抄写传诵，以致洛阳的纸供不应求而价格上涨。

后世以"洛阳纸贵"来赞扬某篇文章或某部著作写得好，风行一时。

Zuo Si（左思，250-305），a writer in Western Jin Dynasty, elaborately composing and weighing every word, spent ten years writing a book on the three capitals of the kingdoms of Wei（魏）, Shu（蜀）, Wu（吴）(《三都赋》). The poems were highly acclaimed by the leading literary figures of his time, and there was a rush to copy it in Luoyang（洛阳）, where Zuo Si lived. As the paper was soon in short supply there, the price rose.

Later, the allusion "Paper is expensive in Luoyang" came to be used to praise a well-written and popular literary work.

注：① 赋：中国古代的一种韵文和散文综合的文体。
Descriptive prose interspersed with verse in ancient China.

朝秦暮楚

zhāo Qín mù Chǔ

Serving Qin in the Morning and Chu in the Evening

春秋战国时,秦与楚两国互相敌对,而韩、赵、魏等国时而倾向秦国, 时而又依附楚国, 后来用"朝秦暮楚"比喻人反复无常。

另外, 北宋文学家晁 (Cháo) 补之在他的《北渚 (zhǔ) 亭赋》里有两句话:"托生理于四方, 固朝秦而暮楚。"(我为了谋生而四处奔走,早晨还在秦地,晚上就赶到楚地。)

秦与楚两地相隔很远。这两句述说他奔波跋涉的艰苦劳累。所以"朝秦暮楚"又比喻行踪不定。

During the Warring States Period, the states of Qin (秦) and Chu (楚) were long-term rivals. The other states would ally first with one and then with the other. "Serving Qin in the morning and Chu in the evening" was used to describe a fickle or disloyal person.

Another source of the phrase is an essay by a Northern Song Dynasty writer Chao Buzhi (晁补之 1053-1110), in which he complains that to earn a living "I am rushing to serve Qin in the morning and Chu in the evening," meaning leading a vagrant life.

东床

dōng chuáng

东床快婿

dōng chuáng kuàixù

坦腹东床

tǎn fù dōng chuáng

Sprawled in the East Wing

此典出自古代小说集《世说新语》。

晋代的王羲 (xī) 之是中国古代有名的大书法家。这里是他的一则逸事①。

有个官员派人到丞相王导家去选女婿，王导让来的人自己到东厢房里去任意选择。这个人回去说："王家的青年人都不错，但听到有人去相亲，都有意表现得温文尔雅，矜 (jīn) 持做作，不太自然；只有一个年轻人敞开衣裳露着肚皮，躺在东床上，好像不知道有这回事一样。"官员说："这正是我要选的女婿。"后来打听到这个年轻人原来是王导的侄子王羲之，就把女儿嫁给了他。

后人用"东床"、"东床快婿"作为女婿的美称。"坦腹东床"则指做了女婿。

The following anecdote is told about the calligrapher Wang Xizhi (王羲之，303-361) of the Jin (晋) Dynasty:

An official sent a servant to the home of Prime Minister Wang Dao (王导) to select one of his sons to be the official's son-in-law. Wang Dao directed him to the East Wing of his house, where the young men lived. Learning of the visitor's mission, the would-be swains quickly donned their best attire and adopted dignified poses—all except one, who remained sprawled on his bed half-naked as if he had not heard about the visitor.

When the servant reported this to his master, the latter

immediately chose the slovenly youth to be his son-in-law. This was a fortunate choice, as the lad turned out to be the renowned Wang Xizhi, Wang Dao's nephew.

Later, "sprawled in the East Wing" or simply "East Wing" came to be used to refer to a son-in-law.

注：① 逸事：多指不见于正式记载的，世人不大知道的有关某人的事迹。

Anecdote.

覆巢之下无完卵

fù cháo zhī xià wú wán luǎn

No Intact Eggs Under an Overturned Nest

　　此典出自古代小说集《世说新语》。

　　孔融(公元 153—208)是汉朝末期人。他是孔子的后代，又是高官和学者。他对曹操（公元155—220）很不满。后来曹操找了借口将孔融逮捕。在逮捕孔融时，家人都很惊恐，但是他的两个儿子一个九岁，一个八岁，却玩耍（shuǎ）如常。孔融向来逮捕他的官员乞求放过他的儿子，这两个孩子却对孔融说："父亲，在翻覆了的鸟巢下还会有完好的蛋吗？"果然这两个孩子也被逮捕，和孔融一起被杀害了。

　　这个比喻后来形容在一个破灭了的团体或家庭中不会有幸存的人。

· This allusion comes from *New Narrations of Social Events* (世说新语).

　　Kong Rong (孔融 153-208) lived in the Eastern Han Dynasty. He was a descendant of Confucius, a senior official and a scholar. He fell foul of the powerful Cao Cao (曹操), who found a pretext to arrest him. When he was arrested, his family was in great terror, but his two sons, one nine years old, and the other eight, kept playing, unperturbed. Kong Rong pleaded with the arresting officers to spare his sons. But the two boys said to him, "Father, can there be intact eggs under an overturned nest?" Sure enough, the two boys were also arrested and slain together with Kong Rong.

This saying later came to be used to denote that when a party of family is destroyed no one connected with it can survive.

口若悬河

kǒu ruò xuán hé

A Waterfall of Words

若:好像。 Like, as if.

晋朝的郭象知识丰富,善于清谈①。同时期的清谈家王衍称赞说:"听郭象谈话好像瀑布流水,长久不停。"

后世因此以"口若悬河"来比喻讲话滔滔不绝。

In the Jin (晋) Dynasty the philosopher Guo Xiang (郭象) was very adept at talking on philosophical topics. One of his contemporaries, Wang Yan (王衍), said, "When I listen to Guo Xiang talking, I feel that his speech is like a waterfall of words!"

Later, the phrase "a waterfall of words" came to be used to describe talking on and on in a flow of eloquence, or keeping up a constant flow of words.

注:① 晋朝的士人和官员多喜欢谈论以道家思想为主的观念,名为清谈或清言。

It was a fashion among the literati and officials of the Jin Dynasty to indulge in empty talk on philosophical subjects derived mainly from Taoism. Such discourses were called "refined idle talk."

青眼

qīng yǎn

Black Glances

青睐

qīnglài

白眼

báiyǎn

White Glances

三国时的阮籍 (公元 210—263) 能做青眼①和白眼②。见俗客就用白眼对着人家。只有对着他赞许的人，才用黑眼珠看人。

青睐的意思也同青眼。

后世以青眼和青睐表示对人的重视、赞许；白眼表示对人的轻视、反对。

Ruan Ji (阮籍 210-263 B. C.), a scholar of the Three Kingdoms Period could see with the whites of his eyes as well as the pupils. He showed the whites of his eyes to unwelcome visitors, and his normal, black pupils to those whom he liked or had a good opinion of.

Hence the phrase "the whites of the eyes" (白眼) came to mean scorn, disgust or exclusion; while "black glances" or "the black of the eye" (青睐) means favor, fondness, approval or appreciation.

注:① 青眼:黑眼珠在中间，正视。

Looking squarely at. *Qing* (青) means black here, and not blue as in modern Chinese.

② 白眼:眼睛朝上或向旁边看，现出白眼珠，是看不起人的一种表情。

Casting a sidelong glance to show superciliousness.

江郎才尽

Jiāng láng cái jìn

Mr. Jiang Has Exhausted His Talents

江郎即南朝文学家江淹，他少年时就以文章作得好而有名，当他做县官时，有一天晚上宿在城外，梦见有人给他一枝五色笔，从此他的文辞越来越华丽。十多年后，有一天他又梦见一个美男子，他对江淹说："我有一枝笔在你这里许多年，可以还给我了。"江淹从怀中掏出笔还给他，从那以后，江淹再也写不出好的诗句。人们说他才尽了。

后世以"江郎才尽"形容某人文思减退，才力不如从前。

Mr. Jiang was Jiang Yan (江淹 444-505), a scholar during the period of the Northern and Southern Dynasties. He was already famous for his well-written articles when young. When he was a magistrate of a county, he dreamed that he was given a splendid writing brush. Thenceforth his works became more and more exquisite and elegant. Ten-odd years later, he dreamt that a handsome man appeared to him. The vision said, "You have kept my writing brush for many years. Now you ought to return it to me." Jiang Yan gave the writing brush back to the man. After that he never wrote anything to match his former works. People said that Jiang Yan had exhausted his talent.

Later, "Mr. Jiang has exhausted his talents" came to be used to describe a man whose inspiration is failing, and his imagination declining.

红绳系足

hóngshéng jì zú

Feet Linked by Red Cords

月下老人

yuè xià lǎorén

The Old Man in the Moonlight

　　这是唐代一部文学笔记中的故事。有人给一个名叫韦固的人提亲。双方约好第二天在一个庙前见面，韦固那一夜兴奋得睡不着，天不亮就到那个庙前去了。他看见一位老人坐在庙前石阶上，靠着一个口袋，就着月光翻着一本簿(bù)册。韦固问老人那是什么书，老人说是掌管天下人婚姻的书。韦固又问口袋里有什么，老人说口袋里装的是红绳，用来拴系夫妻的脚。应成夫妻的人一经用红绳连在一起，即使是仇家或相距遥远，也终必成婚。他还说韦固与第二天要见面的女子也早已系上了红绳。以后韦固的这门亲事果然成功了。

　　后世用"红绳系足"来祝贺婚姻美满。用"月下老人"、"月老"等指主管婚姻的神，也成为媒人的代称。

These allusions come from a Tang Dynasty fantasy.

A man named Wei Gu (韦固) was to be introduced to his prospective bride in front of a certain temple. Unable to sleep with excitement the night before the rendezvous, he arrived at the temple before dawn. There, in the moonlight, he saw an old man sitting on the temple steps with a mysterious bag and a book. He asked what they were, the old man replied that the book was a register of all the marriages in the world, and the bag contained red cords used to link the feet of couples who were destined for each other. Once the cords were fastened, he said, the couple would definitely be married, even if their families were hostile to the matches or if they lived far apart from each other.

Then the old man assured Wei Gu that a red cord had already been tied to his and his bride-to-be's feet. Sure enough, the betrothal was carried out that day, and the couple lived happily ever after.

Later, the phrase "feet linked by red cords" came to signify a happily married couple. A matchmaker or the god who arranges marriages came to be referred to as the "old man in the moonlight."

阮囊羞涩

Ruǎn náng xiūsè

Mr. Ruan's Bag Feels Ashamed

囊:口袋。 Bag.

晋朝的阮孚到会稽（Guìjī）①去游玩，带着一个黑布口袋。有人问他袋子里装的是什么，他回答说："只有一个钱看守口袋，以免空着会使口袋羞涩。"

后世以"阮囊羞涩"表示穷乏、贫困。

Ruan Fu (阮孚) of the Jin Dynasty went on a trip to Huiji, carrying a black cloth bag. When someone asked him what was in it, he answered, "There is only one coin to keep the bag company, so as not to make it feel ashamed of its emptiness."

Later, people used the saying, "Mr. Ruan's bag feels ashamed" to imply being short of money.

注：① 会稽：地名，在今浙江省。
Huiji, in the present Zhejiang Province.

司空见惯

sīkōng jiàn guàn

A Common Sight to the Sikong

司空:古代官名。　An ancient senior official title.

此典来自唐朝孟棨（qǐ）所著的《本事诗·情感》。

唐朝的司空李绅有一次设宴招待著名诗人刘禹锡，席上有歌妓劝酒。刘禹锡当场做了一首诗，说这些歌妓都很美，而司空经常看见她们所以觉得很平常。

后世用"司空见惯"来表示某件事常见，不足为奇。

This allusion is taken from *Poetic Sentiments* by Meng Qi (孟棨) of the Tang (唐) Dynasty (618-907).

The poet Liu Yuxi (刘禹锡) was once invited to a banquet by the Sikong Li Shen (李绅). When a troupe of young songstresses came on to liven up the banquet, Liu composed a poem on the spot, praising the girls' beauty. But the Sikong was unimpressed, as he saw them often and regarded them as a common sight.

Later, the phrase "a common sight to Sikong" came to mean something quite common and not at all out of the ordinary.

请君入瓮

qǐng jūn rù wèng

Please Get Into the Vat

此典出自《资治通鉴》①。

武则天（公元 624—705）在位时有两个酷吏周兴和来俊臣，他们用种种可怕的酷刑来迫使犯人承认罪名。

后来有人告发周兴与人谋反。武则天密诏(zhào)②来俊臣逮捕和审问周兴。来俊臣将周兴请来，问他有什么好办法使犯人招供。周兴说只要把一口瓮烧烫，把犯人放进去就没有不招的。来俊臣于是叫人烧烫了一口瓮，这时才对周兴说有人告他谋反，请他进瓮里去，周兴吓得立即承认了罪名。

后世用"请君入瓮"来形容自己设计的害人办法被别人用来害自己。

This allusion is taken from *The General Review for Ruling*.

In the reign of Tang Dynasty Empress Wu Zetian (武则天 624-705), there were two tyrannous officials named Zhou Xing (周兴) and Lai Junchen (来俊臣), who were ingenious at inventing cruel tortures.

When Zhou Xing was accused of plotting a rebellion, Wu Zetian secretly instructed Lai Junchen to arrest him. Lai Junchen invited Zhou Xing to a banquet, during which he asked him what was the best method of making a prisoner admit to a crime. Zhou Xing said that the best method was to nake an iron vat red-hot, and then put the prisoner in it. Thereupon, Lai Junchen ordered a vat to be heated. When his was done, he said to Zhou Xing, "You are accused of plotting a rebellion, so please get into the vat." Zhou Xing admitted his guilt immediately.

Later, the expression "Please get into the vat" came to be used to describe a plot to frame or harm others which misfires.

注:① 《资治通鉴》是由宋朝司马光主编的编年史。

The General Review for Ruling (资治通鉴) was compiled in the Song (宋) Dynasty (960-1279), with Sima Guang as the chief-editor.

② 诏:告诉,多指上告下。

Instruct, usually by the superior to the inferior.

梨园

lí yuán

Pear Orchard

此典出自《新唐书》。

唐朝皇帝李隆基（公元 685—762）爱好音乐，会作曲，也会演奏乐器。他挑选了三百个青年人和许多宫女，让他们住在长安城内的一个梨树园里，由李隆基亲自教他们演奏音乐，他们被称为"皇帝梨园弟子"。

后世对歌舞戏曲艺人泛称"梨园弟子"，称戏剧界为梨园。

This allusion is taken from the *New History of the Tang Dynasty*.

Emperor Li Longji （李隆基 685-762） of the Tang Dynasty loved music. He himself could play several kinds of musical instruments as well as compose music. He selected 300 young men and palace maids and settled them in a pear orchard in the capital, Chang'an （长安, present-day Xi'an 西安）. The Emperor taught them in person to sing and play musical instruments. They were called "the emperor's pear orchard pupils."

Later, the term "pear orchard" came to refer to operatic circles, and opera performers were called "pear orchard pupils."

安乐窝

ānlè wō

The Cosy Nest

这个典故出自《宋史》。

宋代有一位哲学家邵雍,家里很穷,住的房子很破烂,但是他安于贫穷,生活得很愉快。他自称"安乐先生",称他的住房是"安乐窝"。

后世以"安乐窝"称舒适安静的住所。

This allusion is excerpted from the *History of the Song Dynasty*.

In the Song（宋）Dynasty（960-1279）, there was a philosopher named Shao Yong（邵雍）. He was poor and lived in a tumble-down hut. But he was quite at ease in poverty and lived happily. He called himself "Mister Peace and Happiness（安乐先生）" and his hut "The Cosy Nest"（安乐窝）.

Later, a comfortable and quiet residence came to be called "the cosy nest."

黄粱一梦

huángliáng yī mèng

A Golden Millet Dream

此典出自唐代小说《枕中记》。

有个姓卢的书生进京赶考。在邯郸的一个旅店里遇见一位道士吕翁。卢生抱怨自己穷困。吕翁就从袋中掏出一个枕头给卢生，说："你枕这个枕头睡觉，会让你称心如意的。"那时旅店主人刚开始蒸黄粱米饭（小米饭）。卢生睡下后很快进入梦乡。在那里娶了一位姓崔的女郎。崔氏美丽而且很富有。卢生考中了进士，后来做了十年宰相。他有五个儿子，都做了官。他的亲戚都是门第很高的富贵大户。他活到八十多岁才死。但是，当他一觉醒来时，店主人的黄粱米饭还没有蒸熟呢！卢生诧（chà）异地说："难道是一场梦？"吕翁笑着说："人世间的事情也都和这差不多。"

后世以"黄粱一梦"来比喻虚幻的事情或欲望的破灭。

This allusion comes from a Tang (唐) Dynasty story.

A young man named Lu (卢) on his way to the capital to take the official examination stopped at an inn in Handan (邯郸). There he met an old Daoist named Lü (吕). When the young man complained about his poverty and hard life, the old man took a pillow out of his bag, handed it to Lu and said, "Sleep on this pillow, and you will enjoy what you wish." At that time, the inn-keeper began to cook millet. The young man rested his head on the pillow, fell asleep and began to dream. In his dream, he married a beautiful maiden, who was also very rich. Later Lu acquired the highest acdemic degree. After a series of rapid promotions, he was appointed prime minister, and held that post for ten years. He had five sons, who all reached high official ranks. He had a dozen grandsons. All his children and grandchildren married into noble clans. He enjoyed a long life of over 80 years. However, when he woke up, the host's millets was still in cooking. He wondered, "Was all this but a dream?" The old man smiled and said, "Things in this world are just like that."

Later, "a golden millet dream" came to be used to describe the evaporation of illusions.

南柯一梦

nán kē yī mèng

Southern Branch Dream

柯：树枝。 Tree branch.

此典出自唐代小说《南柯太守传》。

有个人叫淳于棼，家住在广陵，他家院子南边有一棵古槐树，枝干很长大。他在生日那天喝醉了酒睡在树下，梦见到了大槐安国。他娶了那国的公主，当了二十年南柯太守，生了五男二女，享尽了荣华富贵。后来与敌人打仗打败了，公主也死了，他就被免官遣送回家。一觉醒来时，他看见家里的佣人正在扫院子，太阳还没有完全落山，他喝剩下的酒还在那里。于是他就在槐树下面找，看到一个洞穴，他梦中的大槐安国，原来就是槐树下面的蚂蚁洞。

后世以"南柯一梦"指做梦或比喻虚空一场。

This allusion comes from a Tang Dynasty novel titled *The Story of Nan Ke Taishou.*

Chunyu Fen (淳于棼) of Guangling (广陵) got drunk on his birthday and fell asleep under a huge and ancient Chinese scholartree. He dreamed that he journeyed to the Great Kingdom of Huai'an (大槐安国 literally, "peaceful scholartree"). There he married the king's daughter, was appointed prefect of Nanke (southern branch) for 20 years, had five sons and two daughters and enjoyed great wealth and prestige. Later, leading an army against the kingdom's enemies, he was defeated. Soon afterwards, his royal wife died, and he was dismissed from his post and banished from the kingdom.

When he awoke he found his servant sweeping in the courtyard, the sun lingering overhead and wine dregs still in his cup. He looked at the base of the tree, and there, under the southern branch, he found a hole which ants used as their nest: that was what he had dreamed as the Great Kingdom of Huai'an!

Later, a "southern branch dream" came to be used to mean a fond dream or illusory joy.

只许州官放火，不许百姓点灯

zhǐ xǔ zhōu guān fàng huǒ, bù xǔ bǎixìng diǎn dēng

Magistrates May Set Fires But Commoners May Not Even Light Lamps

宋朝有个叫田登的人做汴（Biàn）州的州官，忌讳别人提他的名字。因为"登"与"灯"同音，于是全州的人都把"灯"叫做"火"。

正月十五元宵节之夜，当地有点花灯习俗，叫做"放灯"。官府却贴出告示说："本州依例放火三日"。

后来人们用"只许州官放火，不许百姓点灯"形容统治者可以胡作非为，而老百姓却连正当活动的自由都没有。

In the Song (宋) Dynasty there was once a magistrate of Bian (汴) Prefecture named Tian Deng (田登), who made the uttering of his name by others taboo. This meant that the common people could not speak of "lamps (灯)", but instead had to call them "fire (火)".

As the Lantern Festival approached, on the 15th day of the first lunar month, the authorities in the prefecture put up a notice allowing the people to light lanterns for the festival. But, because "lamps" was taboo, they had to use "fire" instead. So the notice read, "According to traditional practice, fires may be set for three days in this prefecture."

Later, the allusion "Magistrates may set fires but commoners may not even light lamps" came to be used to mean that the ruling class can indulge in any kinds of excesses, but the common people are not even allowed to pursue their ordinary activities.

冰人

bīng rén

The Iceman

此典出自《晋书·索紞(Dǎn)传》。有个官员梦见自己站在冰上和冰下的人说话。他去找索紞解梦。索紞告诉他，冰上为阳，冰下为阴①，他与人隔冰说话是说阴阳事，这个梦是他将要为人说媒的征兆，所说的婚事到冰化时就会完成。这个官员起先不相信，但是不久当地太守就来托他为儿子说媒，他只好去办。结果婚事说成了，到第二年仲春②太守的儿子就完婚了，和索紞的预言完全一样。

后世便称媒人为冰人。

This allusion is from "The Biography of Suo Dan" in *The history of the Jin Dynasty* (晋书).

An official once dreamed that he stood on a frozen pond and spoke with a person under the ice. The official asked Suo Dan, a learned soothsayer, to interprete his dream. Suo Dan told the official that above the ice was *Yang*, while under it was *Yin*. A conversation through the ice meant a dialogue between *Yang* and *Yin*. So the dream was an omen that the official would become a matchmaker, and the marriage would take place when the ice melted. The official was sceptical at first, but soon afterwards he was asked to find a bride for the son of the local governor. He did as he was asked and, just as foretold by Suo Dan, the marriage took place in spring, following the melting of the ice.

Later, a matchmaker was called an "iceman (冰人)".

注：① 阴阳：中国古代关于事物两面性的观念，阳代表向日、雄性、正面；阴代表背阴、雌性、背面。

Yang （阳） and *Yin* （阴） are traditional Chinese concepts of the two opposing principles in nature; *Yang* represents positive, bright, masculine, while *Yin* negative, shady, and feminine.

② 仲春：中国的春季一般为三个月，仲春是春季的第二个月。

Spring in China usually covers three months. Zhongchun is the second month of spring.

东窗事发

dōng chuāng shì fā

East Window Plot

南宋奸臣秦桧①要谋害岳飞②，曾在东窗下与妻子王氏密谋。

秦桧死后不久，他的儿子秦熹也死了。王氏为死者设祭。并派一方士到阴间去探访。方士看到秦桧、秦熹和秦桧的帮凶万俟卨（Mòqí Xiè）都带着铁枷在受苦。秦桧对方士说："烦你捎个口信给我夫人，说东窗下的事情败露了！"

后世以"东窗事发"来比喻阴谋或罪恶败露。

Qin Hui (秦桧), a prime minister of the Southern Song (南宋) Dynasty (1127-1279), once plotted with his wife under the east window of their mansion to assassinate General Yue Fei (岳飞). Both Yue Fei and his son were slain.

Later, not long after Qin Hui died, his son died also. His widow held a memorial service for the two of them and sent a necromancer to the nether world. There he saw Qin Hui, his son and their accomplice in the murder of Yue Fei all in chains. Qin Hui said to the necromancer, "Please tell my wife that the east window plot has seen exposed."

Later, the allusion "east window plot" came to mean that a conspiracy has been unmasked.

注：① 秦桧：曾为南宋宰相19年，主张与屡次进犯的金国讲和。他杀害了抗金名将岳飞，贬黜（biǎnchù）了所有的主战将领，是中国历史上臭名昭著的奸臣。

Qin Hui, prime minister of the Southern Song Dynasty for 19 years, notorious for killing Yue Fei and banishing other patriotic generals in order to capitulate to the invading barbarian State of Jin.

② 岳飞:南宋时抗击外族侵略者的民族英雄。

Yue Fei, a famous patriotic general of the Southern Song Dynasty.

推敲

tuī qiāo

Push – Knock

唐朝诗人贾岛,常常骑着驴吟诗,遇见大官也不回避让路。有一次他又骑着驴吟起诗来:"鸟宿池边树,僧敲月下门。"他想把"敲"字改为"推"字,又拿不定主意,就在驴背上反复做着推和敲的动作,不觉冲进了京兆尹①、文学家韩愈的仪仗队。韩愈手下人把他带到韩愈的马前盘问,贾岛如实回答。韩愈想了很久说:"敲字较好。"就与他一起谈论起诗来。后来两个人成了好朋友。

后世用"推敲"表示反复研究、考虑措辞,又引申为仔细考虑问题和事情。

The Tang (唐) Dynasty poet Jia Dao (贾岛) was once riding on a donkey chanting poems and oblivious of the other people on the road.

While he was murmuring two lines of one of his poems: "鸟宿池边树;僧敲月下门。" (The birds perch in the trees by the pool; A monk is knocking at the gate in the moon-light). He suddenly thought that he should replace the word 敲 (knock) with 推 (push), but he could not decide which to choose. Lost in contemplation, he made gestures of knocking and pushing. The donkey wandered into the path of a procession escorting the magistrate of the capital, Han Yu (韩愈), a famous scholar and writer. Jia Dao was arrested by the guards and brought before Han Yu. Jia Dao told Han about his problem with the poem. The latter thought for a long time, and then said to Jia that he thought the word *qiao*

(敲 knock) would be better.　Then the two literary men became the best of friends.

　　Later, "push-knock" came to denote pondering intently.

注:① 京兆尹:古代官名。

　　Jing Zhaoyin:　an ancient official title.

绿叶成荫

lǜ yè chéng yīn

Green Leaves Make Fine Shade

　　唐代诗人杜牧在湖州①见到一位老妇人带着一位十几岁很美的少女。杜牧与老妇人约好要少女等他十年，如果他十年不来，少女就可以嫁别人，并且给了老妇人很重的聘(pìn)礼②。然而杜牧过了十四年才再到湖州，这时那位少女已经嫁人三年而且已经生了两个孩子。杜牧惆怅(chóuchàng)③之余写了一首诗《怅别》：

　　　　自是寻春去较迟，不须惆怅怨芳时；
　　　　狂风吹尽深红色，绿叶成荫子满枝。

　　后世以"绿叶成荫"形容妇女结婚和生育子女。

The Tang Dynasty poet Du Mu (杜牧 803-852) once went to Hu (湖州) Prefecture. There he met an old woman leading a very beautiful young girl. Du Mu made the old woman promise that the girl would wait for him for ten years. After that, if he did not come to marry her, the girl would be free to marry somebody else. Then Du Mu gave the old woman a large sum of money as his betrothal gift and left. But 14 years passed before he returned. By then, he found that the girl had been married for three years and had already given birth to two children. In his sorrow, Du Mu wrote a poem called, "Melancholy of Separation":

In the quest for spring I met delay.

No need for sad resentment of the flowery season.

The winds have blown away the deep crimson.

Now the green leaves make fine shade,

And the boughs are laden with fruit.

Later, "green leaves make fine shade" came to be used to describe a woman who has married and become the mother of many children.

注:① 湖州:在今浙江省北部。

  Hu Prefecture: in the northern part of modern Zhejiang Province.

② 聘礼:订婚时,男家向女家下的定礼。

  Bride price: betrothal gifts from the bridegroom's to the bride's family.

③ 惆怅:伤感,失意。

  Disconsolate; melancholy.

红娘

Hóngniáng

Hongniang

红娘是元代剧本《西厢记》中的一个角色。故事说，已故崔宰相的遗孀（shuāng）①带着儿女住在一个庙里，有一个书生张珙（Gǒng）也住在这个庙的西厢房里。张珙在庙里遇见了崔家的女儿莺莺，二人互相仰慕。这时一个强盗听说崔莺莺貌美，就带部下包围了这个庙，要强娶莺莺，如果不允就要杀死庙内所有的人。在这种情况下，崔夫人许诺如果有人能救莺莺不落入强盗之手，就将莺莺许配给此人为妻。张珙写了一封信托人带给他的朋友——一位驻地不远的将军，请求援助。将军带兵打败了强盗，救了所有的人。但是这时崔夫人又不肯将莺莺许配给张珙了，只许他们以兄妹相称。于是他们通过莺莺的侍女红娘传递情诗、信件，安排他们见面，最终二人结合了。

现在根据这个故事常称媒人为红娘。

Hongniang (红娘) is a character in the play *The Story of the Western Chamber*. The widow of a high official resided in a temple with her daughter and son. A young scholar called Zhang Gong (张珙), the hero of the story, was lodging in a room in the west wing of the same temple. Zhang Gong met Cui Yingying (崔莺莺), the daughter of the widow, in the temple, and they fell in love. An outlaw who had heard about the beauty of Yingying led his band to surround the temple, declaring that he wanted to marry

Yingying; otherwise he would kill everybody in the temple. The widow promised that if anybody could save Yingying from the outlaw, she would betroth her to him. Zhang Gong wrote a letter asking for help from a friend who was a general stationed nearby. The general led his army to the rescue and defeated the outlaw, and saved the besieged people.

But the widow broke her promise, and refused to betroth Yingying to Zhang Gong, only permitting them to address each other as brother and sister. So the lovers relied upon Hongniang, the maid servant of Yingying, to pass love poems and letters between them. Hongniang arranged for them to meet, and finally brought them together in marriage.

Later, "Hongniang" came to be used to refer to a matchmaker.

注：① 遗孀：某人死后，他的妻子称为他的遗孀。
　　Widow.

刘姥姥进大观园

Liú lǎolao jìn Dàguānyuán

Granny Liu in the Grand View Garden

　　这个典故来自清代著名小说《红楼梦》①，大观园是做高官的贾家居住的地方，园内富丽繁华。刘姥姥是一位农村的贫穷老妇人。由于她是贾家的远亲，所以到大观园来求接济。贾家的老夫人厌倦了日常生活，想听到一些新鲜事情，于是就留刘姥姥在大观园里住几天。刘姥姥没有见过富贵人家的生活，也没见过那里的许多东西，所以闹了不少笑话。

　　现在用"刘姥姥进大观园"这句话形容知识贫乏的人见到了许多没见过的东西而大开眼界，或是穷人接触了富人的生活而不知所措。

　　This allusion comes from the famous Qing (清) Dynasty novel *Dream of Red Mansions*.

　　The Grand View Garden (大观园) was the residence of the wealthy and powerful Jia (贾) family. Granny Liu (刘) was a poor peasant woman who was distantly related to the Jias. She came to the Grand View Garden to ask for assistance.

　　Madame Jia, the head of the household, was bored with her daily life, and wished to hear about something fresh. So she asked Granny Liu to stay for a few days. Granny Liu, as a country bumpkin, made many clownish mistakes in her new and opulent surroundings.

　　Later, this allusion came to be used to describe a person of humble status overawed by someone else's opulence and sophistication.

注:① 《红楼梦》是清代曹雪芹 (? —1763) 所写的长篇小
　　　说。描写做高官的贾家的兴衰及贾宝玉和他的表
　　　妹林黛玉的爱情悲剧。

　　This novel was written by Cao Xueqin. It describes
　　the rise and fall of the Jia family and the tragic love
　　story between Jia Baoyu and his cousin Lin Daiyu.

中国历史朝代年表

夏	公元前 21 世纪—前 16 世纪
Xia	21st-16th century B. C.
商	公元前 16 世纪—前 11 世纪
Shang	16th-11th century B. C.
西周	公元前 11 世纪—前 771 年
Western Zhou	11th century-771 B. C.
东周	公元前 770—前 256 年
Eastern Zhou	770-256 B. C.
春秋时代	公元前 770—前 476 年
Spring and Autumn Period	
	770-476 B. C.
战国时代	公元前 475—前 221 年
Warring States Period	
	475-221 B. C.
秦	公元前 221—前 206 年
Qin	221-206 B. C.
西汉	公元前 206 年—公元 8 年
Western Han	206 B. C. -8 A. D.
新	公元 9—23 年
Xin	9-23 A. D.
东汉	公元 25—220 年
Eastern Han	25-220 A. D.

三国	公元 220—280 年
The Three Kingdoms	220-280 A. D.
魏	公元 220—265 年
Wei	220-265 A. D.
蜀	公元 221—263 年
Shu	221-263 A. D.
吴	公元 222—280 年
Wu	222-280 A. D.
西晋	公元 265—317 年
Western Jin	265-317 A. D.
东晋	公元 317—420 年
Eastern Jin	317-420 A. D.
南北朝	公元 420—589 年
The Southern and Northern Dynasties	
	420-589 A. D.

南朝

The Southern Dynasties

宋	公元 420—479 年
Song	420-479 A. D.
齐	公元 479—502 年
Qi	479-502 A. D.
梁	公元 502—557 年
Liang	502-557 A. D.
陈	公元 557—589 年
Chen	557-589 A. D.

北朝

The Northern Dynasties

北魏	公元 386—534 年
Northern Wei	386-534 A. D.
东魏	公元 534—550 年
Eastern Wei	534-550 A. D.
西魏	公元 535—556 年
Western Wei	535-556 A. D.
北齐	公元 550—577 年
Northern Qi	550-577 A. D.
北周	公元 557—581 年
Northern Zhou	557-581 A. D.
隋	公元 581—618 年
Sui	581-618 A. D.
唐	公元 618—907 年
Tang	618-907 A. D.
武周	公元 684—704 年
Wu Zhou	684-704 A. D.
五代十国	公元 907—960 年
The Five Dynasties and Ten Kingdoms	
	907-960 A. D.
北方五代	
The Five Dynasties in the north	
梁	公元 907—923 年
Liang	907-923 A. D.
唐	公元 923—936 年
Tang	923-936 A. D.
晋	公元 936—947 年
Jin	936-947 A. D.

汉	公元 947—950 年
Han	947-950 A. D.
周	公元 951—960 年
Zhou	951-960 A. D.

南方十国是十个同时或相继的短暂地方政权。

The Ten Kingdoms in the south were contemporary or successive transient local regimes.

北宋	公元 960—1127 年
Northern Song	960-1127 A. D.
南宋	公元 1127—1279 年
Southern Song	1127-1279 A. D.
辽	公元 938—1125 年
Liao	938-1125 A. D.
金	公元 1115—1234 年
Jin	1115-1234 A. D.
元	公元 1271—1368 年
Yuan	1271-1368 A. D.
明	公元 1368—1644 年
Ming	1368-1644 A. D.
清	公元 1636—1911 年
Qing	1636-1911 A. D.
中华民国	公元 1912—1949 年
The Republic of China	1912-1949 A. D.

后　记

　　这本小书原来是要由我的已故表兄何泽人先生写的，但是由于他的健康状况越来越差，最后不得不停止工作，他就把这件事嘱托给我，虽然我和何泽人先生一样是技术人员，过去很少写文艺作品。但是由于长期以来对中文和英文的文学作品都十分爱好，于是便鼓起勇气涉入了这个领域。希望我的工作没有辜负我所怀念的表兄的嘱托，并且有助于促进外国朋友和海外华人与我们民族之间的互相了解。

周苓仲
1996 年 7 月 7 日

Postscript

This book was originally the endeavor of my late cousin Mr. He Zeren, whose work on it was interrupted by ill-health. He thereupon entrusted it to me, though I am a technician by profession, just as my cousin was, and had little experience of literary work. Our long-standing interest in Chinese and English literature, however, encouraged me to venture into this domain. I hope that my efforts have not betrayed the trust of my beloved cousin, but will coutribute to promoting mutual understanding between the English-speaking people and the Chinese people.

Zhou Lingzhong
July 7, 1996

图书在版编目（CIP）数据

典故100：汉英对照 / 周苓仲，何泽人编著．-北京：华语教学出版社，1998.8
（博古通今学汉语丛书）
ISBN 978-7-80052-522-3

Ⅰ．典⋯ Ⅱ．①周⋯ ②何⋯ Ⅲ.对外汉语教学－语言读物
Ⅳ. H195.5

中国版本图书馆CIP数据核字（1998）第10616号

博古通今学汉语丛书

典故100

*

©华语教学出版社有限责任公司
华语教学出版社有限责任公司出版
（中国北京百万庄大街24号　邮政编码　100037）
电话：(86) 10-68320585　68997826
传真：(86) 10-68997826　68326333
网址：www.sinolingua.com.cn
电子信箱：hyjx@sinolingua.com.cn
新浪微博地址：http://weibo.com/sinolinguavip
北京密兴印刷有限公司印刷
1999 年（34开）第 1 版
2012 年第 9 次印刷
（汉英）
ISBN 978-7-80052-522-3
定价：22.00元